'In our politically turbulent age, new a
faithful practice of Christian citizensh
both democratic and authoritarian s
the Middle East. This excellent collect
challenging and biblically-rooted po
Christian citizens everywhere.'

– Dr Jonathan Chaplin, Director at Kirby
Laing Institue for Christian Ethics

'Topping headlines in today's news are reports of the persecution
of Christians in the Middle East and other parts of the world.
Many Christians who are able to flee are leaving their homes to
escape danger. This tragedy requires serious investigation of its
roots and causes. What better place to begin (or continue) the
search for understanding than this book on Christian citizenship
in the Middle East. It does more than assess the multi-dimensional
crisis. Its authors point constructively to ways Christians can hold
fast to their faith while making the wisest decisions possible to
exercise their citizenship.'

– James W. Skillen, Ph.D., Duke University, president
(retired), Center for Public Justice, Washington, D.C.

'This book provides a provocative set of reflections on an important
and timely theme: Christian citizenship as a response to the crisis
arising in the Middle East. It begins a conversation that is essential
to the preservation of pluralism in the Middle East that also extends
to our own western societies.'

– Paul S. Rowe, Professor of Political and International
Studies, Trinity Western University

'Since Jesus raised a denarius and instructed his incredulous
bystanders to "render unto Caesar what is Caesar's" but "to God
what is God's", Christians have labored to understand and to practise
a kind of dual citizenship. The faithful, Christian political witness
is on trial today, hardly more so than in this book's focused region
of the Middle East, where followers of Jesus continue to live "under
Caesar's sword". This is why Christian Citizenship in the Middle East
is an urgent book, not just for scholars of Jesus' homeland, but for
disciples on political pilgrimage all throughout the world, under
many Caesars, owing many obligations – some perhaps proper
patriotism, others needing vigorous resistance. This book is an
indispensable guide for such a time as this.'

– Robert Joustra, Associate Professor of Politics & International
Studies, Redeemer University College (Toronto, Canada)

CHRISTIAN CITIZENSHIP IN THE MIDDLE EAST

Divided Allegiance or Dual Belonging?

Edited by MOHAMMED GIRMA
and CRISTIAN ROMOCEA

Foreword by Paul S. Williams

Thanks for your service to His Kindom! Girma

Dear Line, With my best wishes. Cristian

Jessica Kingsley *Publishers*
London and Philadelphia

Material from *Between Kin and Cosmopolis* (Biggar 2014) used by permission of Wipf and Stock Publishers. www.wipfandstock.com

First published in 2017
by Jessica Kingsley Publishers
73 Collier Street
London N1 9BE, UK
and
400 Market Street, Suite 400
Philadelphia, PA 19106, USA

www.jkp.com

Library of Congress Cataloging in Publication Data
A CIP catalog record for this book is available from the Library of Congress

British Library Cataloguing in Publication Data
A CIP catalogue record for this book is available from the British Library

ISBN 978 1 78592 333 3
eISBN 978 1 78450 648 3

Printed and bound in Great Britain

MIX
Paper from
responsible sources
FSC
www.fsc.org   FSC® C013056

*Dedicated to Christians facing religious
persecution in the Middle East*

CONTENTS

CONTENTS

FOREWORD

Paul S. Williams

For many of us perhaps the most concrete expressions of citizenship arise on those relatively rare moments when we vote in elections or brandish our passports at international borders. On such occasions we may be particularly focused on such matters as the kind of society in which we wish to live, the gratification that arises from the rights that our citizenship in a particular country bestows on us, or the sudden awareness of our status as foreigners as we join the lengthy queue at passport control.

These examples highlight the connection that citizenship makes between each of us and a particular political and territorial community – a particular set of neighbours. It is a connection that establishes a relationship of allegiance and rights, which in the modern world has become highly formalized and foundational. To be stateless – without citizenship – is one of the most extreme forms of marginalization and alienation from human society possible because it likely means that we are (or are about to become) not only materially poor and isolated, but also lack the right to work to support ourselves or to move around to find work and associate with whom we wish. Citizenship is thus basic to our creaturely existence as embodied, located and relational beings.

In this thought-provoking collection of essays, the authors explore the nature of citizenship from a Christian perspective. Christian faith requires unconditional allegiance to Jesus Christ and grants the rights of heavenly citizenship. A particular question for Christians is thus how to navigate the claims and freedoms of these two kinds of citizenship, the heavenly and the earthly. Does Christian citizenship create, in the words of the volume's subtitle, a divided allegiance? Are Christians only loyal citizens when the territory of which they are a part has been Christianized?

Or does genuine Christian loyalty transcend territory? After all, as Girma highlights at the outset of the volume, Christian citizenship is transnational and universal in character, forming bonds that extend outside and beyond those of the territorial state. Biggar presses this point by asking whether there should be any loyalty at all to the nation-state. In marked contrast to the historically normal situation in which religious adherence and territorial belonging are assumed to be coterminous, should we not rather think of ourselves as 'citizens of the world'? From these provocative starting points both authors develop rich accounts of what a distinctively Christian relationship to earthly citizenship might be.

The focus on the Middle East is powerful, contemporary and salutary. Any minority group existing inside a dominant culture faces challenges, and Christians are no different. There is an extraordinary temptation to secure the rights of earthly citizenship either through religious and political takeover of a territory, or to assimilate and acquiesce to its norms in order to preserve the citizenship benefits of belonging. Diab's historical review powerfully reveals the division and conflict that arise through the complex interplay of these factors while also providing a nuanced account of Christian contribution to and involvement in the Arab civilizations of the Middle East that have been dominated by Islam for over 1,400 years. Awad argues that, in the Syrian context especially, it has been tempting for church leaders to mimic their Muslim equivalents by opportunistically seeking sectarian political advantage for the Christian community and thereby undermining genuine Christian witness.

These reflections on the Middle East, as instructive as they are, become even more powerful for Western readers in the context of the refugee crisis and large-scale migration. Strine examines how the huge movements of peoples into Western countries, many of them Muslims, provoke the Western church to examine its own attitudes toward citizenship. Ryan picks up the theme in the final essay, noting the irony that the idea of a religiously homogenous nation-state is a legacy of the religious wars following the Reformation – and one that damages genuine Christian witness. These two authors consider respectively the stance of the Church and the role of international law in promoting an environment that truly welcomes the stranger.

Throughout this volume the extraordinary contribution of Scripture to a Christian vision of citizenship becomes evident. The biblical witness, both in the trajectory of the Old Testament and the settled foundation of the New Testament, shifts the theological framing of citizenship from the identification of religion and nation exemplified by political Israel, to that of exile. It was in exile that the Israelites finally learnt the extent of their calling to be a blessing to the nations, by seeking the welfare of the pagan city in which they found themselves. Exile is the theological context for mission in the New Testament, so that as citizens of heaven believers are encouraged to maintain exemplary public conduct in order to bear witness to God's character and love. As becomes clear in this volume, this biblical perspective on citizenship is both historically and theologically remarkable, even unique. For what Christianity requires is not simply a transfer of allegiance from one people or tribal group to another, but rather a fundamental relativizing of the very notion of citizenship itself. Those who profess to follow Jesus Christ are given an identity and a belonging that is 'not of this world' yet from this identity they are to function as exemplary citizens of whatever group they happen to belong to. In the upside-down world of the Kingdom of God, Christian citizens become foreigners wherever they are and whatever earthly rights they possess, yet precisely because of this 'other-worldly' identity, become capable of being exemplary citizens in any nation-state, no matter its religious character.

The issues raised and ably discussed in this volume are profoundly relevant to the global Church at a time when both nation-states and religious fundamentalisms are re-asserting themselves. If we are truly to serve the purposes of God in our generation, we will need to reflect deeply on these matters and to act prayerfully. This book is an invitation to such an engagement.

Professor Paul S. Williams
Chief Executive, British and Foreign Bible Society

INTRODUCTION

Cristian Romocea, Oxford, UK

The Arab Spring and consequent violent reactions infamously known as the Arab Autumn and Arab Winter, which included regime collapse, political turmoil, instability, violence, sectarian struggles, divisiveness and religious extremism, threatened the fate of all minority religious groups and denominations in the region. The socio-political effects included public demonstrations associated with the Arab Spring in Tunisia, Egypt, Morocco and Saudi Arabia, public riots and regime collapse in Libya and Yemen, or more recently, the devastating war in Syria. Moreover, it created a climate for the development of Islamic fundamentalism, whose violent effects were felt particularly among the Christian populations in the Middle East. This book aims to explore the concept of citizenship from a biblical point of view, with special focus on what the Bible has to offer Christians in these contexts who want to play an influential role as citizens in rebuilding peace and social and political harmony in the Middle East.

This publication is designed to profile the Bible in timely and relevant public discourse in various cultures and contexts by exploring the positive contribution of the Bible in the history of a particular society. In our previous book, *Democracy, Conflict and the Bible*, we showed the contribution of the Bible to democratization, and how it inspires justice, reconciliation and peace.[1] In this book, the editors have invited Western and non-Western voices to reflect on the biblical vision for citizenship from their particular angles.

What is involved in the notion of citizenship? For a long time, the answer to this question was relatively clear: citizenship symbolized

---

1   Romocea, C. and Girma, M. (eds) (2015) *Democracy, Conflict and the Bible*. Swindon: Bible Society.

a rigid relationship between a given nation, state or territory, and its residents who are entitled to rights and duties. In the era of globalization it has, however, become more difficult to achieve a clear understanding of this notion since seemingly contrasting characteristics, applied together or separately, have tended to define citizenship in new and more complex ways. Citizenship is an ambiguous and underexplored concept particularly in relation to religion. In contexts where a certain religious group represents a minority, defining their citizenship proves especially difficult. On the one hand, minority religious group members living in such contexts are born and raised in concrete cultures and states. They cannot see themselves entirely outside their historical situatedness. The awareness of citizenship based on historical situatedness comes with its sense of civic responsibilities and duties required to be carried out in a given society. On the other hand, their religious commitment means that they are often marginalized and not fully embraced by their society. This pushes them into looking for a conception of citizenship which transcends their historical situatedness, often defined by tapping into notions from within their own religious tradition.

The outworking of such a scenario is a situation in which, in some matters, Christians in places such as the Middle East, for example, can forge a better solidarity with Christians outside their culture than with non-Christians in their own culture. The challenge faced by Christian minority groups in these contexts is apparent; they will be pushed to the margins in their own culture because of their religious commitment, whilst cultural and geopolitical difference can be a formidable challenge for them when attempting to forge a meaningful solidarity with Christians from outside their countries. The fundamental questions of this book then will be: what is the biblical vision of citizenship? Does or should espousing a notion of citizenship based on a religious tradition assume insulating oneself from civic duties and responsibilities in a concrete state? What are the possible ways in which Christian minorities can exercise a positive contribution to the rebuilding of a harmonious society without repudiating their own religious identity? While tackling these questions, the book will touch on and discuss values that undergird citizenship, such as patriotism, duty, social harmony and integrity.

What is the relationship between the Bible and citizenship to a Christian? The Bible speaks with ambiguity about citizenship in both the Old and New Testaments; there isn't a clear conceptual articulation of the notion, instead we find various iterations influenced by context, geography, as well as political and cultural factors. In the Old Testament (OT), the normative shape of citizenship in Israel is given by the Torah. YHWH[2] stands in the centre of the political process and impinges on every facet of the social and political. Israel's self-representation is a political theology in which God is intensely engaged with questions of power, policies, and practices of good distribution and access. As Walter Brueggemann stresses, all Israel's politics is theologically marked and all its theology is politically inclined.[3] The prophetic literature is where we see Israel recognizing the reality of public power on the ground which culminates in the destruction of Jerusalem, because of its claims of absolutism. With YHWH at the centre of its political imagination, the citizens of Israel are empowered to imagine an alternative political economy of covenant, to practise it in their own lives, and to testify to that contrasting alternative in the life of the world.

In the New Testament (NT), we find references to citizenship in Jesus' teaching on attitudes to political power. From the temple tax story (Matthew 17.24–27), we learn about the biblical view on paying taxes. As Oliver O'Donovan stressed in reference to this episode, 'now that the King is present, citizens of the kingdom are free from the constraints of the empire, but purely as a concession Jesus and his disciples will pay taxes so they'd not be perceived as rebels'.[4] Moreover, we find that Jesus' reply to the Pharisees on the question of paying taxes to Caesar (Matthew 22.16–21) provides the basis for a defence of human dignity and prime responsibility to God. It's also a summons to recognize the citizens' limits to their obligation. All things belong to God, and they should be returned to Him; liberty is not Caesar's. The most explicit reference to

---

2   The tetragrammaton is the Hebrew name of God transliterated in four letters as YHWH or JHVH and articulated as Yahweh or Jehovah.

3   Brueggemann, W. (2004) 'Scripture: Old Testament.' In P. Scott and W.T. Cavanaugh (eds), *The Blackwell Companion to Political Theology*, Blackwell Companions to Religion, p.9. Oxford: Blackwell.

4   O'Donovan, O. (1999) *The Desire of the Nations: Rediscovering the Roots of Political Theology*, p.92. Cambridge: Cambridge University Press.

citizens' subordination to authorities in the NT is where Peter counsels Christians, addressed as resident aliens and visitors, to defer to institutions and honour the emperor, but as 'free men' and moreover as 'God's servants' (1 Peter 2.13–15). Christian citizens are thus urged to respect the appointed political order while at the same time recognizing that the judgments within the community of Christ are to be resolved by a different set of criteria in view of the cross and the future judgment of God upon humanity (1 Corinthians 6ff.).

Romans 13 contains the most disputed discussion on citizenship in the New Testament. Paul here speaks in continuation of his claims about Israel; just as Christ's victory was the same victory promised to Israel over all nations, that of a YHWH-filled covenantal and humanized social order over God-denying empires, so the human authorities are claimed for obedience to Israel, chastened and reduced to the familiar functions that were once ascribed to Israel's judges. For Paul, the 'prevailing authorities' he describes in Romans 13 is a term alluding to the angelic character assigned to national governments in ancient Hebrew culture; in the context of the victory of Christ, who has overcome all principalities and powers through his death and resurrection, state authorities are already subjugated to Christ. The authorities must judge, but Christian citizens too are now subject to the divine wrath ministered through the secular government, not because of fear but because of respect to God's purposes based on conviction.

Thus perceived, the biblical vision of citizenship can inform Christians living in any state as to how to approach the demand for civil duties and responsibilities without a loss of their religious identity. In the first chapter, Mohammed Girma goes deeper into this subject by articulating a Christian vision of citizenship that will enable believers to perform their civic duties better when they live as a religious minority in a state. Girma's articulation of a Christian vision of citizenship taps into the ancient Athenian concept of the 'city' and how this has influenced the social and political arrangements of the world of the biblical authors. In attempting to provide two specific biblical examples of the appropriation of citizenship, Girma introduces us to Daniel, a noble Jewish youth from Jerusalem and the hero of the OT Book of

Daniel, and to the Apostle Paul, the teacher of the gospel of Jesus Christ to the first-century world. These two biblical personalities share common characteristics; they were both led by their call and mission into encounters with the political establishments of their time. Moreover, they both shared a Jewish identity which was culturally in tension with the predominant Babylonian and Roman empires, and cosmologically in opposition with their religious values. These examples enable Girma to argue that the biblical vision for citizenship is one that chooses neither withdrawal from civic engagement nor immersion or assimilation but a critical engagement with the political establishment. Thus perceived, the Christian living as a minority in a country is best placed to tell the Christian story of human flourishing and thus offer a critical support to the state, fulfil civic duties and responsibilities, all without the loss of her identity.

In the second chapter, the focus shifts from Christian minority citizens to the biblical and theological requirement for all Christians in relation to their country or nation. Nigel Biggar invites us to explore what it means to espouse as citizens the Christian *agape* exemplified by Jesus' teaching and example without running the danger of becoming oblivious to local and national bonds. Drawing on the examples of Jesus and the Apostle Paul in the New Testament, Biggar challenges us to a hermeneutic that does not reject patriotism and loyalty to one's nation in the name of an unconditional and indiscriminate love for humanity in general. Juxtaposing a cosmopolitan Christian identity which insists on the equal value of all human individuals sharing a common origin and destiny to loyalty and patriotism that gives precedence to local and national communities, customs and institutions, Biggar argues for a Christian concept of creatureliness of human being that can justify a preference for benefitting near neighbours over distant ones, compatriots over foreigners. However, Biggar does not see cosmopolitanism and national diversity as unnatural; instead, he argues for such diversity as a natural necessity which leads to cross-national reflective engagement and mutual learning. For Biggar, the doctrines of creation, the Incarnation of God, and the Trinity offer a clear theological basis for human diversity, once more affirmed in Christ's message about a kingdom of all nations, as opposed to a world-empire. The moral obligation to serve the common human good compels us to respect and promote what is good for one's nation, rather than what it demands; true patriotism is not uncritical.

Whereas in Chapter 2 Nigel Biggar spoke about the moral obligation of a critically assumed patriotism, Chapter 3 offers us an example of genuine and self-critical patriotism. The author, Najib George Awad, reflects on whether Christians will still be able to play an influential role in recreating social harmony in a post-war Syria and peaceful Middle East. He argues that while the Christians in the Middle East in general, and in Syria in particular, may not cease to exist in the region in the future, they will probably lack any tangible presence or influential role in society, and their contribution will not influence the stability of the recreated Arab society characterized by tolerance, safety, peace, neutrality, impartiality and citizen rights. Although the author seems to think that the Bible and the Christian tradition has resources within itself to support such values in a society, he fears that the present church leaders' poor record of political neutrality and impartiality will hurt their potential contribution to the future stability. Tacit support of the Assad regime, support for the distorting propaganda against the civil demonstrations and the public rebellion in the country, self-victimization and demonization of the Muslims (e.g. Syria), or involvement in sectarian clashes for power and monopolization by all means (e.g. Lebanon), all seem to affect the Christian witness and solidarity with the broader society over the long term. The solution for the recreation of harmonious future societies in the Middle East envisaged in this chapter is linked to the establishment of secular states that will ensure human rights are observed, that citizens benefit from rights and protection, and where people are no longer divided along confessional, ethnic or religious considerations.

In Chapter 4, Issa Diab offers us a critically hopeful view of the future of Christianity in the Middle East based on an assessment of the historical record of Christianity's continued presence and positive contribution to the Arab civilization from Byzantine times through to the establishment of Islam in the seventh century, the renaissance of the Arab civilization, and until today. The author contends that in spite of the difficulties, the Levantine Christianity is still playing its role in the Middle East at the spiritual, human and social levels. Throughout the history of the Arab region, Middle Eastern Christians, inspired by the teachings of the Scriptures, have lived at the intersection of two allegiances: allegiance to their Christian mission, and allegiance to their Middle Eastern citizenship. In a highly informative historical account, the author details the specific contributions of Christians to Arab culture by highlighting the early contribution of John of Damascus and other Christian families to the development of education and religious thinking among Muslim intellectuals of their day. Here we find that the 'classical' culture of the golden age of Islamic civilization was made possible through the numerous translations by Christians into Arabic of literary works of philosophy, science, theology, medicine and astronomy, which influenced the development of sciences and culture in the growing Islamic empire. We furthermore read about the crucial influence of Christian scholars and institutions to the three waves of Arab renaissance of the sixteenth to the nineteenth centuries in the cultural, economic and political areas, but also through reforms in women's education, social sciences, literature, linguistics and grammar. The author concludes with a reminder of the effect of the current waves of Islamic fundamentalism on Christian presence in the Middle East: a reduced Christian population, persecution and destruction of churches. However, he contends that Christianity will remain a presence in the Middle East as long as the strength of its citizens is not sought in numbers but in an authentic message of service, love and forgiveness.

In Chapter 5, Casey Strine suggests a range of biblical material relating to migration, providing a basis upon which to outline a Christian approach for responding to the issues surrounding the integration of migrants into host societies. The diverse statements in the Old and New Testaments, the author argues, indicate that both hosts and migrants have obligations to the other group that should promote embracing those from different backgrounds without eliminating enduring differences between them. Furthermore, the Bible outlines a view of Christian identity that supersedes national identity without eliminating its role; this relationship has consequences for Christians among host groups. Finally, the duty of hosts must demonstrate the sort of self-sacrificial love that engages even with those who may pose a threat to oneself, the very model of self-sacrificial love embodied by Jesus himself. To make this case, the author proceeds in four steps. First, he offers a discussion of what the Bible says about migration, attending to the most relevant statements about the duties of both hosts and migrants. Second, there is a brief discussion of the critical points regarding what it means for a Christian to be a citizen, with particular focus on how the concept of Christians as dual citizens in this world impacts their role as hosts for migrants. Third, this material is synthesized into a view of what a Christian approach to integration comprises, before fourth and finally discussing a potential biblical example of this approach.

In the last chapter, Ben Ryan argues that there is a need to question the idea that citizenship is only defined by the needs of the state. Instead, he proposes that a Christian basis for citizenship would see a far greater focus on human dignity and a rights-based approach. Conceptions of citizenship (particularly as they concern migrants) have become largely rooted in debates over the interests of states, and the need to defend the homogeneity of the national community from internal breakdown and external threats. The tactics adopted by nation-states to serve their own interests have taken the conception of citizenship further and further away from the interests of individuals or the defence of human dignity. The author argues that for Christians in the Middle East, who live as a minority community, this raises particular challenges. Resonating with the call for the establishment of a secular state that will ensure human rights are observed discussed in Chapter 4, Ryan suggests here that a Christian contribution to debates over citizenship needs to establish the underpinning values and moral basis by which citizenship is to be addressed. At present the rationale behind state approaches to citizenship has become entirely focused on the interests of states over individuals. Economic demands, the security agenda and a demand for assimilation have overtaken all other factors. Making a Christian case is to challenge that development, and the basis of a citizenship based on a 'methodological nationalism' which sees all political identity as consisting wholly within the borders of the nation-state. Only by challenging that model can a Christian vision of citizenship for a new age begin to be built on the basis of rights, responsibilities and human dignity over and above the particular interests of states. This chapter therefore first explores how the current status quo has formed, with state interests and fears over a loss of homogeneity taking preference over other factors. It then proposes the building blocks for a Christian conception of citizenship that start from the principle of human dignity and the need for a rights-based approach.

Where possible, the authors of this book have used practical examples, case studies and incidents demonstrating how the Bible can address citizenship in a specific situation. The straightforward and accessible writing style is suitable for non-specialist readers, whilst being robust and credible for those who are coming from an academic arena. The authors have tried to avoid theological or philosophical jargon (or explain it where it is used) so that the content will be accessible for those whose first language is not English. I hope that you will find the rich content of this book useful and enlightening, as it sheds a new light on a set of contemporary issues that we cannot avoid today.

Chapter One

CITIZENSHIP
A Christian Conception
Mohammed Girma, Swindon, UK

CITIZENSHIP: THE ATHENIAN ORIGIN

Citizenship is one of those aspects of being human which is often hotly debated, jealously guarded and carefully maintained. I shall start its conceptual analysis by way of discussing its origins. Etymologically, the word 'citizen' comes from the Latin term *civitas* referring to a collective body of equal members in polity of a given (national) boundary.[1] Perhaps the best starting point to elucidate the notion is briefly unpacking the notion of the 'state' in ancient Greece. State for them was a commonwealth, a republic or even a constitution. This is very different from the modern understanding of the state. In other words, in modern conception, the state is an independent entity as an institution. It could be aloof and often antithetical to the interest of the individual. For ancient Greeks, there was no such autonomy between citizens and the state. The membership in the state and the state as an institution were closely interpenetrated.[2]

Citizenship in this ancient setting was a membership in the *polis*. The Greek idea of *polis* has two different but inseparable layers of meaning. First, it can be interpreted as a physical settlement, or a modern equivalent of city-state. Inhabitants of this settlement include adult males, women, children, 'free foreigners' and even slaves. The second dimension of *polis* is stricter precisely because it denotes a civic involvement of

1   Clarke, P.P. (2013) 'Citizenship.' In P.P. Clarke and A. Linzey (eds), *Dictionary of Ethics, Theology and Society*. Abingdon: Routledge.
2   Ehrenberg, V. (1968) *From Solon to Socrates: Greek History and Civilization during the 6th and 5th Centuries BC*, pp.88–89. London: Methuen.

koinonia (a tight family-like community), which excludes women, children and foreigners.

The principal criteria to become a member of *polis* in the later sense were being an Athenian by birth, reaching the age of 18, getting registered in the same village, or *deme*, where one's father belonged.[3] However, there were also other provisions by which one could become a citizen. Adoption is an example. Through the process of adoption, a child becomes a member of the deme of his adopted father. This means that the child loses his right of inheritance from his natural family. In reverse, however, the child loses his citizenship in case of reunion with his natural family.[4] In the registration process each citizen undergoes careful inspection by senior members of the *deme*. Once the application of an individual is successful, his names are inscribed in the list kept by the *deme*. This denotes that an individual can now not only enjoy legal adulthood, but also has the right to fulfil his obligation of, for example, attending, speaking and voting in the popular assemblies. The duty of citizenship in the *polis* also entails performing religious rituals such as worshiping, participating in Athenian cults and festivals.[5]

What about foreigners? Foreigners were allowed to live in the *polis* – the city-state. However, the Athenian law had identifiable boundaries between foreigners, resident aliens and slaves. Unlike citizens, the aforementioned pockets of society did not have a legal basis to enjoy certain rights. For example, they could not hold a public office, own land or marry an Athenian woman. Furthermore, if foreigners wanted to trade in the public market, they had to pay extra taxes. They had very limited access to the justice system. However, they could not enjoy the same legal rights and protection as male Athenians.[6] Even though they were excluded from political assemblies, they were required to fight in the army alongside the citizens. Slaves did not have an identity of their own. They were the responsibility of their masters. Even in cases of homicide, an Athenian life had higher value compared

---

3   Manville, P.B. (2014) *The Origins of Citizenship in Ancient Athens*, p.7. Princeton, NJ: Princeton University Press.

4   Harris, E.M. (2016) 'A note on adoption and deme registration.' *TYCHE – Contributions to Ancient History, Papyrology and Epigraphy 11*, 1, 5.

5   Manville (2014), p.8.

6   Zelnick-Abramovitz, R. (1998) 'Supplication and request: Application by foreigners to the Athenian polis.' *Mnemosyne 51*, 5, 554–573.

with that of a foreigner or a slave. A person who killed an Athenian was tried in the high court on the Areopagos and faced the death sentence if convicted, while a person who killed a foreigner was tried in a lower court in Palladion and sent to exile, if convicted. [7]

So being an Athenian citizen means more than sharing the *polis*. Citizens are expected to exhibit a behaviour, feeling and attitude that are attendant upon them. The virtues of good citizens in Athens include discretion in private dealings with neighbours, courage in battle, love for beauty and wisdom, prosperity with moderation, grace and versatility, respect and obedience to divine and human order and authority.[8]

The practice of virtue has direct implications for the distinction between public and private life. The Athenian principles of virtue put public good over private interest. Even then, the private and the public lives are inseparably intertwined. The philosophy behind this is that citizens can only live a life of fullness when they live honourably both in and around the *polis*. Part of the reason is that Athens was a predominantly a 'face-to-face society' led by oral culture. These two elements – face-to-face social interaction coupled with oral tradition – made popular participation in political affairs necessary.[9]

To pull this part together, citizens in ancient Athens are at the same time the subjects of the authority of the city-state and the creators of it. They create the rules and regulations with a conviction that they must obey them to be able to enjoy the fruits of justice, peace and harmony. It is important to stress that the state is not an all-powerful independent entity with the power that impinges upon the individual. Instead, it is a hub built by citizens for them to have a tight and family-like interaction with each other. Active civic participation, by making sure the rules and regulations are properly implemented and by practising civility and virtues, is a hallmark of citizenship. However, behind the democratic-looking façade is a class system that reflects the hierarchical relationship not only between citizens and foreigners, but also between citizens (such as between adult men on the one hand, and women and children on the other).

---

7   Athenaion Politeia 57.3.
8   Manville (2014), p.15.
9   Manville (2014), p.15.

CITIZENSHIP IN THE BIBLE: CHARACTER ANALYSES

For a variety of reasons, the notion of citizenship in the Bible is not as consistent and clear as in the Athenian culture. For one thing the Bible covers the Middle East, the Graeco-Roman world and beyond. This is coupled with the fact that the Bible covers a large span of time and a range of political paradigms. Yet another factor is that, even during the Graeco-Roman domination of the world, the privilege of citizenship was limited to cities. For example, Jesus did not have citizenship because he was not born in a city. Moreover, the residents of monarchies are generally seen as subjects, not citizens.[10] There is another dimension to the lack of clear-cut conceptualization of citizenship in the Bible: namely, the intention of the biblical authors during the writing was not to provide conceptual articulations of anything. As Walter Brueggemann rightly points out, their writings were driven by the impulse to give a testimony about God.[11] The notion of citizenship is no exception.

Therefore, one plausible orientation to understand the biblical conception of citizenship, perhaps, is paying attention to the rhetorical unity of the biblical writings. The underlying pattern pervading the bulk of biblical literature would help us to find and follow a golden thread. However, the task of sifting through a plethora of historical epochs, socio-political contexts, authorial intentions, literary systems and theology goes beyond the scope of this chapter.

For this part, however, I opt to employ a different approach. I will select two individuals – Daniel from the Old Testament and the Apostle Paul from the New – and analyse their characters (the way they conducted themselves in the political realm) and teachings. These biblical personalities are appealing candidates for this purpose because, for one, they are two figures whose call and mission brought them into direct contact with the political establishments of their times. For another, they performed their mission with an awareness that they were living in two (sometimes conflicting) cultural and cosmological horizons.

---

10   Pilch, J.J.A. (2012) *Cultural Handbook to the Bible*. Grand Rapids, MI: William. B. Eerdmans Publishing.

11   Brueggemann, W. (1997) *Theology of the Old Testament*, p.119. Minneapolis, MN: Fortress Press.

Culturally, they had to manage the tension between their Jewish identity and their presence in the Babylonian and Roman empires. Cosmologically, the nature of their presence and activities in these empires demanded reconciling their religious values – or 'heavenly citizenship' – with their concrete presence under the empires which were hostile to their faith.

Daniel: Constructive disruption

The author of the book of Daniel (whoever this might be) depicts Daniel as a young and bright Jewish man living in exile after the Babylonians besieged Jerusalem around 650 BCE and took him and his friends captive. Babylon was a city in the part of the world known as Mesopotamia. The area includes modern Syria and Lebanon. While the name Babylon in Akkadian language means 'get to the gods', it denotes a strong religious flavour permeating the city's life, politics and economy.[12] It was seen by some as a city of eternal abode, the centre of the world and a city of wisdom.

There are some striking similarities and differences between Babylon and Athens. Both were city-states. Moreover, they both took egalitarianism and consensus as hallmarks of their social fabric. However, these social values emanated from different political structures. Namely, in the Athenian *polis*, these values came about as a result of conscious and intentional negotiation between members of the community to protect the welfare of the citizens, whereas the Babylonian version of egalitarianism was a cultural product. To wit, evidence shows that, first, Babylonians grew in their appreciation of equality and consensus because of persistent face-to-face communication and limitations of geographical expansion. Second, the key feature of their economy was not based on land ownership, which could potentially produce land-based elites. Rather, it was based on control over labour which in nature was not hierarchical.[13] Third, even though kings held the ultimate power, they were practically isolated and distant from city life.

---

12   Stefanovic, Z. (2007) *Daniel: Wisdom to the Wise: Commentary on the Book of Daniel*, p.22. Nampa, ID: Pacific Press Publishing.
13   Stone, E. (1997) 'City-states and their Centres.' *The Archaeology of City-States: Cross-Cultural Approaches*, pp.15–26. Washington, DC: Smithsonian Institution Press.

In contrast to Athenians, Babylonians had a fluid cosmological structure, which had direct implications for their social structure. They believed that humans are created to serve gods. However, while their gods were created in the image of humans, kings could elevate themselves to the level of gods and, as exhibited in the book of Daniel, even require worship. In the Babylonian social structure, the king sits on the top of the pyramid and is subsequently followed by nobles, citizens, soldiers, civil servants, debt slaves and captives.[14] It is interesting to see citizens come next to the nobles in the ranking. Nevertheless, the level of their influence and the kind of role citizens played in the political system is not entirely clear. However, given the fact that the king and nobles were placed in the upper social ranks, it is not hard to imagine that the social and political influence of the citizens was much less significant compared with that of the Athenian *polis*. The book of Daniel itself shows that the king, at times, required absolute obedience from citizens.

However, there seems to be a better chance of social mobility (upward and downward) in the Babylonian system, compared with that of the Athenian *polis*.[15] For example, if a child was born of slave parents, he remained a slave. However, if one of the parents were married to a free person, the child could become a free citizen. On the other hand, if one was unable to pay a debt, he could sell his family member as a slave to pay the debt.[16] The story of Daniel and his three friends shows an element of meritocracy to their social structure where even a captive could climb to the highest ranks of the society based on what he could contribute.

Let us now have a closer look at Daniel as a person (or character in the narrative). Daniel came to Babylon with an entirely different worldview. In his Jewish cosmology, God is perceived as the Creator, Builder and Excavator.[17] Human beings are created in God's image (whatever that means) to serve God rather than vice versa. In the Jewish political system, kings are appointed by God. And as such, they are directly accountable to God, and by

---

14   Wang, T. (2003) *History of the World*, pp.25–26. New York: iUniverse Inc.
15   Stone (1997), p.25.
16   Wang (2003), p.28.
17   Hoffmeier, J.K. (1983) 'Some Thoughts on Genesis 1 & 2 and Egyptian Cosmology.' Available at www.academia.edu/2118837/Some_Thoughts_on_Genesis_1_and_2_and_Egyptian_Cosmology, accessed on 20 March 2017.

extension, to the people. Even though accountability runs through it, the structure between spiritual and material order is constant. Humans are to be treated equally because the God of Israel is the God of justice. Injustice, in Jewish understanding, is more than wronging a fellow human. It is wronging God; or to use Nicholas Wolterstorff's words, 'depriving God of that to which he has a right [...]'.[18] God's demand for justice as his right and the rights of humans, therefore, are the basis of Daniel's understanding of social structure.

How did Daniel reconcile the conflict between his worldview and that of the Babylonians and became a productive member of Babylonian society? First, Daniel read the horizon and saw history as a divine vehicle moving forward to fulfil God's ultimate purpose. What comes with such a vision is the conviction that universal events have their assigned places in God's cosmic design. For Daniel, therefore, the drama of the present time, the summit of history, is the birthplace of the 'Son of Man', whose empire will not pass away.[19] Exile was a major setback in Israel's life, and as a young and promising individual, this comes to Daniel with a sense of loss. Such loss, as Andreea Ritivoi aptly describes, includes, but is not limited to, the loss of home which means the familiarity of daily life, loss of occupation which is the value of someone to the society and loss of language which means naturalness of reactions, simplicity of gestures and spontaneity of sentiments.[20] However, Daniel perceived his presence in Babylon as divine providence rather than historical accident. He was able to see hope amid crisis because he had wisdom and spiritual awareness to sense God's upper hand. He conducted himself in the public role with acute understanding of God's sovereign control of history. Eschatological positivity (impending and ultimate divine victory), rather than the present crisis, became the guiding light of his actions.

Second, Daniel did not employ a utopian approach in his encounter with the Babylonian religion and political system. Instead, he sought opportunities within the existing social and

---

18 Wolterstorff, N. (2008) *Justice: Rights and Wrongs*, p.93. Princeton, NJ: Princeton University Press.

19 Lacocque, A. (2015) *The Book of Daniel*, p.10. Eugene, OR: Wipf and Stock Publishers.

20 Ritivoi, A.D. (2002) *Yesterday's Self: Nostalgia and the Immigrant Identity*, p.13. Lanham, MD: Rowman & Littlefield Publishers.

political structure to set his feet and lead a life of integrity. Fluidity in the Babylonian social structure means that there were opportunities to climb the social ladder. Every opportunity, however, brought him into conflict with his religious and cultural identity. For instance, when he was selected for education in the palace, the underlying motivation of the king could have been unlearning him of his religious and cultural values by using education as a tool of assimilation. Living in the palace was another privilege. However, it could have been a way of disconnecting and uprooting him from his upbringing and objectifying Daniel to use him as a tool to the king's own social and political ends. Daniel's approach was to grab the opportunities with both hands and yet to refuse to be objectified. By holding fast to his values, he solidified his position as a prominent individual in the city-state and beyond. He brought sufficient (but necessary) disruption to the Babylonian religious and social order that made him a prominent subject rather than an object. By the way he conducted himself in the public arena, he exhibited, on the one hand, that his values were non-negotiable, and on the other, that he could bring to the Babylonian empire something nobody could offer. Moreover, he showed that his values were the source of his excellence. In the end, despite his Jewish identity and religiosity, he was promoted to the rank of governor of Babylon province and palace official.

Third, Daniel lifted up his fellow captives by making his talents count. Exile – the same holds true for living in minority – is an experience that throws one into the realm of irrelevance. Studies show that people suffering marginalization and cultural dislocation find it very difficult to make their talents count.[21] They constantly hear a voice from the past, and refuse to take good care of their immediate surroundings. They can become obsessed with flying back to their glorious past rather than doing things that are relevant in the here and now. As a result of this, marginalized minorities often face the risk of being disenfranchised. Daniel, however, took a variety of steps which made his new orientation a new home. For one, he treated the political establishment with respect and generosity. He communicated with the king and his officials in a culturally acceptable manner. By doing so, he made

---

21   Ritivoi (2002), p.22.

his surroundings more hospitable for himself and others. His wisdom and spiritual insights helped the king to address big challenges of his time. As a result, he opened doors for Shadrach, Meshach and Abednego to be appointed in 'high positions in Babylon Province' (Daniel 3.49).

Apostle Paul: Internal transformation

Paul undertook his missionary work during the Roman Empire. The organization of the Roman Empire had some similarities with that of the Babylonian Empire. The empire was divided into provinces which had several cities within them. The emperor used to govern those cities through local strongmen.[22] So the empire can be best described as a 'commonwealth of cities' under one emperor. City-states enjoyed some autonomy as they used to grant citizenship to their inhabitants who fulfilled certain requirements. In contrast to the Athenian *polis*, the inhabitants of city-states were represented by 'town councils'.[23] Even though membership of the city council was restricted to the wealthiest members of society, the assembly was open to all adult male citizens who satisfied the minimum requirement of property ownership.

Paul was a man of complex religious and cultural identity. He described himself as a Roman citizen (Acts 22.24–29), a Jew from Tarsus in Cilicia (Acts 21.39) and a Hebrew sprung from Hebrews (Philippians 3.5). He was a zealous member of the Pharisees who, later on, became a follower of Christ. Tarsus, the place he grew up, was a city of flourishing economic and cultural life. According to some sources, it produced numerous (mainly Stoic) philosophers, rhetoricians and poets.[24] Even though the Jews in Cilicia were a Diaspora group, they maintained their synagogue in Jerusalem for pilgrims attending festivities (Acts 6.9). It is not entirely clear if Paul had full citizenship in the city in the same mould as a wealthy property owner, or whether he was referring to his place of origin and emotional attachment to it. One theory is that,

---

22 Howe, S. (2002) *Empire: A Very Short Introduction*, p.47. Oxford: Oxford University Press.
23 Howe (2002), pp.44–45.
24 Schnelle, U. (2005) *Apostle Paul: His Life and Theology*, p.59. Ada, MI: Baker Academic.

during the imperial period, city-state citizenship was purchased for 500 drachmas. Thus, Paul could have inherited his citizenship from his privileged ancestors who had purchased it previously.[25] What is significant, however, is that being a citizen of Tarsus did not preclude being a Roman citizen. The reason is that Roman citizenship superseded all others, and Paul was a Roman citizen by birth.[26]

Another important aspect of Paul's identity is that he was a city person. The city life pervades his language. His metaphorical constructs of gymnasium, stadium and military orders show that he was at home with city life. It is also clear that he had first-hand experience of a very hierarchical social system in the city. His description of himself as a tent-maker shows that he, perhaps, belonged to a social class somewhere between desperately poor and the lucky few whose source of wealth was agricultural estate.[27] Cities in the Roman Empire were known for hostility between (over)confident aristocrats and poverty-ridden peasants. Cities were accommodative of religious plurality. This, however, came with a price tag. Followers of different religions were expected to reciprocate the 'generosity' of the empire by recognizing the divinity of the Roman gods – especially the emperor, Caesar. Refusing to incorporate the imperial cult was seen as a threat to civil order. On the other hand, for Paul, Christian monotheism was something that could not be compromised.[28]

An important question is: how did Paul reconcile the political ecology of his existence (the Roman Empire) with the world he perceived?

Paul seems to have been confronted with this question when he was in Philippi – one of the colonies of the Roman Empire. It was a burning question for believers there because some had the privilege of their names being written in Rome as members of the commonwealth, and the majority of the believers were subjects of the empire, not citizens. Adding another layer to the complexity was the fact that Christians were persecuted minorities not fully

25   Hengel, M. and Deines, R. (1991) *The Pre-Christian Paul*, pp.6–14. Philadelpia: Trinity Press International.
26   Schnelle (2005), p.60.
27   Meeks, W. (2003) *The First Urban Christians: The Social World of the Apostle Paul*, p.9. New Haven, CT: Yale University Press.
28   Jackson Preece, J. (2005) *Minority Rights* pp.20–21. Cambridge: Polity Press.

embraced by the empire. Paul's response was that their 'citizenship is in heaven', and as such, their ultimate commitment should be promoting the interests of this kingdom (Philippians 3:20).

This should not imply that Paul was subscribing to some form of escapism. His approach is much more nuanced than it appears. In Pauline cosmology, material and spiritual orders have their own peculiar identities. The conflict of interest between the two orders, and the ensuing social and cultural dislocation among the believers, are genuine concerns. The two orders, nevertheless, are not radically disconnected. In fact, political order – the empire in Paul's time – is a divine means (albeit temporary and imperfect) of maintaining order and justice. Therefore, as far as Paul is concerned, the conflict is not innate to the ontology of citizenship. It is an element which crept in as the result of human fallibility. The way to resolve the conflict between the two orders is not by insulating oneself from the material order. It instead is by living a transformed life that aims to redeem the social and political order. In this vein, he, elsewhere, implores the believers to pray for kings and all those in authority so they can rule in peace and tranquillity (1 Timothy 2.2). In the Pauline conception of civic engagement, both confusing religious with civic duties and entirely divorcing them cause theological discord. This is because they create unwarranted dualism which makes redemption unattainable. Redemption works in relationship rather than isolation and escapism. Paul understood the messiness of living in the intermezzo of diverse orders, but he also saw it as a place where redemption would take place.[29]

How Paul conducted himself as a member of the *civitas Romana* was as important as his conceptualization of citizenship. First, Paul was more than a religious preacher; he was also an intellectual and cultural innovator. The starting point of his cultural innovation was aiming for internal transformation. Christians during Paul's time did not have financial muscle; neither did they develop intellectual and cultural resources. Moreover, they did not have many defenders among the elite class, which left their relationship with the Roman Empire unarticulated. So Paul's

---

29   Dockery, D.S. (2008) *Renewing Minds: Serving Church and Society through Christian Higher Education, Revised and Updated*, p.29. Nashville, TN: B&H Publishing Group.

approach to fill these gaps was not employing radical disruption against the empire. Instead, he started with foundational conceptualization of Christians' presence in the empire. The assumption was that any movement of cultural innovation requires generating ideas and knowledge. At the centre of his epistemology was the goodness of the Creation, the tragedy of human imperfection which damaged the good created order and the hope of redemption. The notion of citizenship was not his exclusive focus, but it is this theological framework that explains it. Knowing transformation is most enduring when it penetrates people's imagination and frame of knowledge, Paul then handed over this conceptual understanding to those whose works are concrete and visible. Pastors, fellow missionaries and church leaders were his network through whom he channelled his transformative narrative.[30]

Second, he used his privileged status as a citizen for his own personal protection and to minimize the threat of being scourged. For example, once he was seized by a mob in Jerusalem. Wanting to find out why people seized him, a Roman commander ordered Paul to be taken into the fortress and beaten with a whip. As soldiers were tying Paul up to be beaten, Paul told them that he was a Roman citizen and that it was illegal to beat a citizen before he had been tried in the court. The commander then quickly released Paul, in order not to be found violating the law (Acts 22.24–29).

Third, Paul deployed his understanding of the Roman legal system to expand the scope of his mission in the empire. Besides having a comprehensive grasp of legal protection for citizens, he also knew that citizens could appeal their case to the emperor when they felt they were not fairly treated. In this vein, Paul made an appeal to Caesar and transferred his case from a prosecutor in Caesarea to the imperial court in Rome (Acts 25.10–12). Paul's use of legal protection had a dual purpose. He, from the very beginning, knew that witnessing about Christ to the emperor was an important part of his mission. He deftly transposed the court case from being about himself to being about Christ. As the head

---

30   Davison Hunter, J. (2010) *To Change the World: The Irony, Tragedy, and Possibility of Christianity in the Late Modern World*, p.42. Oxford: Oxford University Press.

of the empire, anything that concerned the emperor was more than the emperor's personal issue. By extension, any confrontation with the king had wider ramifications for the whole empire.

Finally, he allowed his social and cultural heterogeneity to shape his missional imagination. Paul grew up in a united empire with social and cultural plurality within it. He did not see plurality as threatening. In fact, cultural plurality was one of the standings in the political structure of the empire that Paul enjoyed and thrived in.[31] Moreover, his understanding of cultural pluralism became a paradigm for what some would call a 'gentile breakthrough' and justification for the missionary expansion of different geographical frontiers. In Pauline perception, some elements of culture and social structure are not to be rejected only because they are different. They are there to be redeemed and revitalized so they become a vehicle for telling the Christian story.

CITIZENSHIP: CRITICAL ENGAGEMENT

We so far have seen the idea of 'city' running through our discussion. The way it is presented here, city is more than a place of residence. It typifies the society and culture we live in. It is a melting pot of diverse voices, culture and ideological expressions. The city life, despite modern pretensions of neutrality, is value laden. Opposing political persuasions, contradicting ways of life and competing religious groups make the city life. In a (post) modern sense, the city is a place that entertains an imam calling for prayer, an evangelist shouting at the corner of the streets and an atheist bashing Jesus. Furthermore, the concept of city is relevant because the project of globalization is transforming the whole world into a gigantic city. When something happens in New York, economic and political vibration is felt even in tiny towns in Africa.

Let me sharpen the demarcations of city life before discussing the notion of critical engagement. Augustine of Hippo, a fourth-century African theologian and philosopher, discusses 'two cities' rather than one integral city. In his influential book

---

31   Picirilli, R.E. (1986) *Paul the Apostle*, p.7. Chicago, IL: Moody Publishers.

The City of God, Augustine differentiates between the *civitas Dei* and the *civitas terrena* – the city of God and the earthly city. The two cities, according to Augustine, represent two opposing ways of life rather than two actual geographical areas. What separates them is the kind of love they pursue in their course of historical development. Namely, the city of God is driven by the love God made manifest in Christ whereas the earthly city fuels itself with self-love. So the human presence on earth is characterized by constant battle between the two loves.

From his characterization of the cities, it appears that Augustine is promising a sharp dualism between heavenly citizenship and earthly citizenship. Moreover, Augustine depicts Christians living under the Roman Empire as 'sojourners', 'captives' or 'aliens'. Considering the political situation of his time, his rather grim portrayal captures the mood of Christians whose presence in the empire attracted immense hostility. But there could also be a deeper philosophy underpinning his cosmology because, in his pre-Christian life, he adhered to a gnostic religious dualism which pitted 'an evil world against the good world'.[32] Even then, he strongly believed that there should be no hesitation among Christians about keeping in step with civic laws which govern matters pertaining to their existence here and now. His justification is that believers share with others a common existence, and therefore, they ought to positively participate in the common causes of human existence.[33]

We can deduce two points from Augustine's conception of Christians' civic involvement. First, the world in which Christians live might be unfriendly. Hence, he gave an unflattering metaphor of 'captives' and 'aliens' to depict their existence in the empire. Second, he affirms that the solution for the hostility they faced in their social ecology should not be withdrawal from civic life. This is precisely because withdrawal from the world is a theological impossibility. Here is the premise. In Christian theology, as Gover Buijs aptly points out, the God of the Beginning, the Creator of this world, is also the God of the Beyond. To put it differently, the

---

32   Skillen, J.W. (2014) *The Good of Politics (Engaging Culture): A Biblical, Historical, and Contemporary Introduction*, p.51. Ada, MI: Baker Academic.

33   Bourke, V.J. (1958) *Augustine, The City of God*, p.XIX, Ch17, 464. Garden City, NY: Doubleday Image Books.

God of the *civitas Dei* is also the God of the *civitas terrena*. Yes, it is impossible to drag the totality of the Beyond into the here and now. However, something of 'the city of God' must be realized in 'the earthly city' (if these two worlds are interconnected). Hence, it is the tension between being in 'this world but not of this world' that permeates Christian civic participation.[34]

We have to, then, ask: what is a plausible orientation for Christians to play their civic role in good faith?

First, Christian theology has it that believers' presence in the world ought to be saturated by *agape*, selfless commitment. In his article 'Agapé and the Origins of Civil Society', Buijs explains that in pre-biblical Greek tradition *agape* exists as a verb – *agapaoo*. As a verb, the term represents an act of treating someone with respect or lifting up someone. *Agape* in a substantive sense was virtually unknown. The word got its currency when the Septuagint used the same word to express love in the divine paradigm. In a substantive sense, agape can be elucidated as a concrete commitment to someone's flourishing and inviting the beloved to play the role that fits the person. This commitment is extended to the beloved even when the person lags behind.[35] In his book *Love's Philosophy*, Richard White details three major characteristics of *agape*. First, *agape* is spontaneous and unmotivated. It is not driven by self-enrichment and calculated personal gain. It is arbitrary and uncaused. Second, *agape* is indifferent to values. It is drawn to all regardless of one's character, attitude, ability, etc. It does not draw a line between saints and sinners. Third, *agape* is creative. It works to highlight the good of the beloved. It works to find ways to create and foster a conviction of being a valued member of the society.[36]

Let us contrast this to what normally drives the political realm: power. Seeking public office is inseparably linked with the pursuit of power – a force that impinges upon the freedom of the other. By its very nature power is a way of affecting the behaviour of others, by using legal means or military coercion.

---

34 Buijs, G. (2008) 'Agapé and the Origins of Civil Society.' In H. Geertsema, R. Peels and J. van der Stoep (eds) *Philosophy Put to Work: Contemporary Issues in Arts, Society, Politics, Science and Religion*, p.35. Amsterdam: VU University.

35 Buijs (2008), p.23.

36 White, R. (2001) *Love's Philosophy*, pp.129–130. Lanham, MD: Rowman & Littlefield Publishers.

A contrasting metaphor elaborating *agape* in Christian thinking of civic engagement is Incarnation. God is seen in Christian theology as the ultimate epitome of power. He, however, chose a different approach to bring about transformation of human life. Refraining from unleashing a force that trumps human freedom, he chose the road of *kenosis* – emptying himself of power ascriptions and becoming a servant. This nevertheless does not mean that God abandoned his power as a means of affecting others' behaviour. Rather, he reversed the direction of influencing others by using a humble and vulnerable means.

Living a life saturated by *agape* is a moral and political critique that can be directed towards the political establishment that uses power for the purpose of self-enrichment. Morally, the life of servanthood uplifts the poor, under-privileged and the marginalized. By doing so, it brings a new image of what it means to have power. Politically, over and against the vertical arrangement of society, where the heads (or kings) are on the top of the power pyramid, *kenosis* fosters horizontal relationship. *Kenosis* is a process of becoming one of them in order to empower those who are in the margins. This is also an indirect call to sensitize the conscience of the political leaders to take social and economic injustice seriously. The hallmark of the life of *kenosis* is active and intentional highlighting of shared humanity and establishing a strong solidarity with those who are left behind.[37]

Second, combining Christian faith with civic engagement is not a side issue. It is not something we address when we unexpectedly bump into it. Civic engagement is a genuine and integral part of Christian faith. It is important, however, to add a caveat that Christian teaching always maintained the distinction between the state and the church. Even though the state–church relationship is construed differently in Christian traditions, the overarching consensus is that they are sovereign institutions. In other words, the Church, as an institution, should not tamper with the role of the state and vice versa. The argument for this is that the intrinsic purpose of the state is administering justice while the church's identity is defined as taking care of the fideic (faith) aspect of human existence.

---

37   White (2001), p.30.

The institutional differentiation, nevertheless, should not be read into the individual. The individual is more interwoven into different social spheres and institutions, and as such, his presence and activities should reflect this. Dietrich Bonhoeffer and Martin Luther King are the best examples. Bonhoeffer lived and paid the ultimate price for his Christian commitment under the Nazi regime. His cosmology, like that of Augustine, has a semi-dualistic tendency albeit his takes a temporal shape. Namely, the tension and entanglement between penultimate and ultimate shapes the contour of his thinking in Christian engagement. The former shows our existence here and now, while the latter indicates the eschaton. Though there is undeniable tension between the two horizons, they are inseparably intertwined. He illustrates this, in *Ethics*, in a very vivid fashion. 'The hungry person needs bread', Bonhoeffer explains, 'the homeless person needs a shelter, the one deprived of right needs justice, the lonely person needs community, the undisciplined one needs order, and the slave needs freedom'.[38] Bonhoeffer's concern here is not exclusively charitable actions and Christian benevolence; his assertions are unmistakably political as well. In other words, Christian engagement with society should include (and start with) an attendance to physical needs and human rights. However, the motivation for the engagement in the penultimate is innate to eschaton – the ultimate.

Third, biblical precedence shows that Christians should not shy away from seeking their vocation in public life even when they are in the minority. The privilege of public office in the Christian paradigm, however, needs to be taken with a certain mindset. To wit, the office needs to be taken as a tool of spreading *shalom*. *Shalom* is a word with a wide semantic range. It signifies peace between two entities (including between God and humans), prosperity, justice, righteousness, security, friendship, well-being, etc.

There are two fundamental principles which can be drawn from this concept. First, *shalom* is about right relationship. This relationship surpasses human relationship with one another. According to Walter Brueggemann, 'the central vision of world

---

38   Bonhoeffer, D. (2008) *Ethics, Vol. 6*, p.163. Minneapolis, MN: Fortress Press.

history in the Bible is that all creation is one, every creature in community with every other, living with harmony and security towards the joy and well-being of every other creature'.[39] It is a way of being that overcomes strife, quarrel, social tension, mutual suspicion, enmity and war. Another dimension of *shalom* is that it is related to perfection. This description, thus, goes beyond wellbeing in various historical spheres. Here *shalom* becomes a cosmic principle which anchors on divine attribute.[40]

In short, *shalom* is a totality of human flourishing.[41] 'Shalom comes', Wolterstorff argues, 'when we bodily creatures, not disembodied souls, shape the world with our labour and find fulfilment in so doing and delight in its result'.[42] A Christian pursuit of public office strives to be in sync with the divine paradigm of perfection. This is because *shalom* in the divine horizon is blind to the cultural and even religious differences that usually dictate our politics, because it strives to embrace the totality of creation.

CONCLUSION

As indicated at the outset, religion is a diversity dilemma. It is even more so when it is new and followed by a minority. Such a dilemma has a unique ability to create mutual suspicion not only between religious groups, but also between religious groups and the political establishments. The usual way of mitigating inter-religious or political tension is either withdrawal from civic engagement or absolute immersion (or assimilation) into the culture in which we live. Our investigation of the Bible and theology, however, indicates insulation and assimilation are theologically unwarranted. The fundamental reason for this is the unmistakable tension and unbreakable interpenetration between believers' existence in this world and the world to come. One plausible approach recommended here is critical engagement. This starts with a careful reading of the cultural and political horizons.

---

39   Brueggemann, W. (2001) *Peace: Living toward a Vision*, p.13. St. Louis, MO: Chalice Press.

40   Ravitsky, A. (1987) 'Peace.' In A. Cohen and P. Mendes-Flohr (eds) *Contemporary Jewish Religious Thought*, p.685. New York: Charles Scribner's Sons.

41   Anderson, R.S. (2007) *Something Old, Something New: Marriage and Family Ministry in a Postmodern Culture*, p.46. Eugene, OR: Wipf and Stock Publishers.

42   Anderson (2007), p.46.

This enables us to use small but significant openings in the culture to tell our Christian story of human flourishing. Living on the intersection of this world and the world to come with good faith demands integrity and generosity. Integrity helps us to stand up for our ideals, our faith and the values that we hold dear, while generosity opens our eyes to find a ground for solidarity with those whom we think do not share our beliefs and values. This ground, however small, is of critical importance because, for one, it is where our conceptualization can germinate. For another, it creates a platform to build a network of like-minded individuals to spread the story.

Chapter Two

THE BIBLE, CHRISTIANITY AND PATRIOTISM

Nigel Biggar, Oxford, UK

AGAINST COSMOPOLITANISM

In the West, there are some who think that there is no virtue in patriotism or loyalty to one's own nation.[1] Since all human individuals are of equal value, we have no good reason to prefer those who speak our language, share our customs, occupy our patch of the globe, or participate in our political community. Indeed, particular loyalties, whether to family or nation, are vices, moving us to discriminate unjustly against those whom Fate has cast outside the boundaries of our favoured group. Rather, enlightened by the speed and ease of global communications, we should transcend the benighted tribal attachments that have spawned so much human conflict and misery in the past, and embrace a new, cosmopolitan identity.

At first glance there are some obvious reasons why Christians should share this cosmopolitan view. Although Jesus did not cease to identify himself with the Jewish nation, he did distance himself from militant nationalist resistance to Roman imperial domination. We are told explicitly in the Gospel of John that he evaded those who would make him 'king' (John 6.15).

---

1   This view seems to me present even in some reaches of British Government. David Goodhart tells the following story of an exchange over during dinner at an Oxford college in the Spring of 2011: 'When I said to my neighbour, one of the country's most senior civil servants, that I wanted to write a book about why liberals should be less sceptical about the nation state and more sceptical about large-scale immigration, he frowned and said, "I disagree. When I was at the Treasury I argued for the most open door possible to immigration... I think it's my job to maximize global welfare not national welfare"' (*The British Dream. Successes and Failures of Post-War Immigration* (London: Atlantic Books, 2013, p.xxv). I have heard reports of similar sentiments currently held by civil servants in the Department for International Development.

More generally, however, the pacific tenor of his teaching and conduct indicated a vision of God's reign alternative to that espoused by militant nationalism. Moreover, Jesus distanced genuine religious faith from the rites and authority of the Temple in Jerusalem, recognized that it was not the monopoly of his own people, and acknowledged its presence in Samaritans and Gentiles (Matthew 8.5, 27.54; Mark 15.39; Luke 7.3, 23.47). After Jesus' death, Saint Paul further loosened the connection between faith on the one hand, and blood and land on the other. Although he too insisted on maintaining and asserting his Jewish identity, he nevertheless developed an understanding of religious faith that is not oriented toward the particular location of Jerusalem, which transcends ethnicity, and which has no proper interest in the restoration of a Jewish nation-state. Out of such an understanding emerged the transnational religious community known as the 'Church'.

Given these origins, it should not come as a surprise that some interpret Christianity as implying a liberal, cosmopolitan stance over and against a partisan, nationalist one, and as preferring love for humanity in general over love for a particular nation. One expression of this can be found in Richard B. Miller's argument that Christian love for others is properly indiscriminate and unconditional: 'Christianity requires an indiscriminate, unconditional love of others, irrespective of political, social, or national affiliation... Christian *agape*, exemplified by Jesus' teaching and example, is altruistic and cosmopolitan'.[2]

This claim has two main grounds, one biblical and the other theological. The biblical ground comprises those passages in the New Testament where 'natural' loyalty to family is severely downgraded. Among them are those in the Gospels where Jesus is reported as saying that only those who hate their mothers and fathers can be his disciples (Matthew 10.37; Luke 14.26), that those who would follow him must 'let the dead bury the dead' (Matthew 8.22; Luke 9.60), and that his 'family' now consists of those who have joined him in his cause (Matthew 12.46–50; Mark 3.31–35; Luke 8.19–21); and also, by implication, those passages

---

2   Miller, R. (2001) 'Christian Attitudes towards Boundaries.' In D. Miller and S. Hashmi (eds) *Boundaries and Justice: Diverse Ethical Perspectives*, p.17. Princeton, NJ: Princeton University Press.

in the Epistles where Paul recommends virginity or celibacy as a higher good than marriage (1 Corinthians 7).

The theological ground consists of the typically Protestant concept of God's love as showered graciously on every human creature regardless of their moral status – a concept that was most fully developed in the 1930s by the Swedish Lutheran theologian, Anders Nygren. According to Nygren, God's love is utterly spontaneous and gratuitous; it is not attracted to the beloved by any of their qualities (how could it be, since those whom it loves are all sinners?), and it is in no sense beholden to them; it is simply and absolutely gracious.[3] As God loves us, so should we love our neighbours: with a pure altruism that entirely disregards their qualities. It is quite true that Nygren himself was not directly addressing the question of whether or not a certain local or national partiality in our affections and loyalties is justifiable, and that his focus was on the religious relationship between God and sinful creatures. Nevertheless, he made it quite clear that Christians are to mediate to their neighbours the same unconditional and indiscriminate love that God has shown them.[4]

What should we make of these biblical and theological grounds? Do they really imply that Christian love should be oblivious to local and national bonds? I think not. Certainly, the so-called 'hard sayings' of Jesus imply that natural loyalties are subordinate to the requirements of loyalty to God; and that sometimes the latter might enjoin behaviour that contradicts normal expressions of the former. But, given that Jesus is also reported as criticizing the Pharisees for proposing a piece of casuistry that effectively permits children to neglect the proper care of their elderly parents (Mark 7.9–13); and given that, notwithstanding his affirmation and commendation of Gentiles (Matthew 8.5–13, 15.21–28), he apparently maintained his identity as a Jew (Matthew 15.24, 26; John 4.22); there is good reason not to take these 'hard sayings' at face value, and to read them as hyperboles intending to relativize rather than repudiate

---

3   Nygren, A. (1982) *Agape and Eros*, trans. Philip S. Watson, pp.75–81. Chicago: University of Chicago Press. Nygren uses the New Testament word *agape* to designate this radically altruistic kind of love, which he believes to be peculiarly Christian, and to differentiate it from the Greek concept of love as essentially self-serving *eros*. *Agape and Eros* was originally published in Swedish in 1930 (Part I) and 1938 (Part II).

4   Nygren (1982), pp.733–737.

natural loyalties. As for Paul, it is notable that, although he reckoned virginity and celibacy superior, he persisted in regarding marriage as a good. In other words, in spite of his urgent sense of the imminent ending or transformation of the world by God, and of how this revolution of the current order of things would severely strain marital and family ties, Paul never went as far as to say that investment in society through marriage and children should cease. What he thereby implies is that, although the arrival of the world-to-come will involve the transformation of this world and its natural social bonds, it will not involve their simple abolition.

Upon closer inspection, then, the New Testament grounds for supposing Christian love to be properly unconditional and indiscriminate are not at all firm. That is even more so in the case of the theological ground. Certainly, if we take Jesus to be God incarnate, we can infer that the love of God for wayward human beings is gracious – or, to be more precise and specific, forgiving. As I have argued elsewhere, the word 'forgiveness' commonly means two different things. It points to two distinct moments in the process of reconciliation: first, one of 'compassion', and then one of 'absolution'.[5] Compassion is unilateral and unconditional and meets the wrongdoer before he has repented; absolution is reciprocal and conditional and meets him only afterwards. God's love is compassionate in that it sympathizes with wrongdoers in their weakness and confusion and ignorance; and it is absolving in that it is willing to set past injury aside and enter once again into a relationship of trust. But note how limited is the scope of this love: it operates only between an injured party and the one who has done the injury. It is a mode of love, but not the whole of it. Accordingly, it is unconditional and indiscriminate only in part. As compassion, its being offered is not conditional upon the demonstration of repentance, and it is therefore made available indiscriminately to all sinners. As absolution, however, it is only offered in response to an expression of genuine repentance, and therefore only discriminately to penitent sinners.

Since this analysis, with its denial that all of forgiveness is unconditional, might sound counter-intuitive to Christians,

---

5   I have explained my analysis of forgiveness into the two moments of compassion and absolution in several places. One of the most recent of these (2011) is 'Melting the icepacks of enmity: Forgiveness and reconciliation in Northern Ireland.' *Studies in Christian Ethics 24*, 2, 200–204.

especially Protestants, let me offer a brief defence. I have two points to make, one biblical and one empirical. First, in Jesus' paradigm of forgiveness, his parable of the Prodigal Son (Luke 15.11–32), the heartfelt repentance of the son is already fully established before we learn of his father's eager forgiveness:

> When he came to his senses, he said, '...I will set out and go back to my father and say to him, "Father, I have sinned against heaven and against you. I am no longer worthy to be called your son..."' (vv.17–19a)

This he proceeds to do. While it is true that the father is filled with compassion and rushes to embrace him before he has so much as opened his mouth, the very next moment in the story has the son give explicit voice to his penitent intentions: 'The son said to him, "Father, I have sinned..."' (v.21). What this implies, I suggest, is that the parable does not tell a story of simply unconditional forgiveness. Yes, the father's compassion is unconditional. Nevertheless, the son's repentance is a prominent part of the story, and not at all incidental, and that gives us reason to suppose that what follows depends on it.

My second line of defence is empirical and briefer, and invites the reader to reflect on her own experience. Such reflection will confirm, I suggest, that it is unloving and foolish to absolve someone who has shown insufficient awareness of what they have done wrong, both because it forecloses their moral education and growth and because it makes it likely that they will proceed to cause further injury.

Such is my defence of the assertion that God's love, as shown in Jesus and his teaching, is not simply indiscriminate. Let me return now to the larger point: that the kind of love that Jesus mainly models is that which bears on how we should treat those who have wronged us. What it does not bear upon is how we should distribute our limited emotional, physical, temporal, and material resources in caring for the millions of fellow humans who can now claim to be – more or less closely – our neighbours. The argument from God's *agape* to Christian cosmopolitanism does not work.

THE PROPER LOYALTIES OF HUMAN CREATURES

So how should we relate to near and distant neighbours? My view is that Christians should begin their answer to this question by reference to Genesis with its concept of the human being as creaturely. On the one hand this implies basic human equality. If all human beings are creatures of the one God, then they all share a common origin and destiny, and a common subordination. If human creaturehood is then specified in terms of being made 'in God's image', then all human beings are thereby dignified with responsibility to manage the rest of the created world;[6] and each is the subject of a vocation to play a unique part in God's work of bringing the created world to fulfilment. If we add to the doctrine of creation that of universal sinfulness then humans are also equal in the fact (if not the degree) of their sinful condition and so in their need of God's gift of forgiveness, and consequently none has the right to stand to another simply as righteous to the unrighteous.

Given these various kinds of basic equality, each human being owes any other a certain respect or esteem, such that, for example, he will not take the other's life intentionally or wantonly, whatever his national affiliation may be. A Briton cannot regard the life of an Indian or a Chinese person as any less valuable than that of a compatriot, for they too are loved by, and answerable to, God, and they too might mediate God's prophetic Word. But human beings might owe others more than mere respect and a commitment to refrain from intentional or wanton harm. They might also owe them aid. In addition to non-maleficence, that is, they might also owe beneficence. However, whereas we are always able to refrain from harming other people intentionally

---

6   The seminal notion that humankind is made 'in God's image' derives from one verse in the Book of Genesis: 'Then God said, "Let us make man in our image, after our likeness; and let them have dominion...over all the earth"' (1.26). In the history of Christian tradition this phrase has been interpreted in many different ways. However, the interpretation that is closest to the text understands it in terms of the practice of kings in the ancient world of setting up statues of themselves in outlying provinces or having their image imprinted on coinage, in order to represent the presence of royal authority throughout their empire. To be made in God's image, then, is to be made a representative or vice-gerent of God, charged with exercising dominion in God's name over the rest of creation. For a history of the exegesis of Genesis 1.26–27, see Westermann, C. (1984) *Genesis 1–11: A Commentary*, trans. John J. Scullion, pp.147–155. London: SPCK.

or wantonly, we are not always able to benefit them. We may be responsible, but ours is a responsibility of creatures, not of gods; and our creaturely resources of energy, time, and material goods are finite. Therefore, we are able only to benefit some, not all; and there might be some to whom we are more strongly obliged by ties of gratitude, or whom we are better placed to serve on account of shared language and culture or common citizenship. In short, notwithstanding the fact that all human beings are equal in certain basic respects, no matter what their native land, we might still be obliged – depending on the circumstances – to benefit near neighbours before or instead of distant ones.

However, whether near or far, human neighbours are not the only proper objects of our respect and care. So are customs and institutions. Humans come into being and grow up in a particular time, and if not in one particular place and community, then in a finite number of them. A human individual is normally inducted into particular forms of social life by her family and by other institutions, such as schools, churches, clubs, workplaces, political parties, public assemblies. These institutions and their customs mediate and embody certain apprehensions of the forms of human flourishing – that is, basic human goods – that are given in and with the created nature of human being. It is natural, therefore, that an individual should feel special affection for, loyalty toward, and gratitude to those communities, customs, and institutions that have benefitted her by inducting her into human goods; and, since beneficiaries ought to be grateful to benefactors, it is right that she should. We have yet to specify the forms that such affection should and should not take; but that they should take some form is clear.

Why loyalty to the *nation*?

It is proper for an individual to have affection for, feel loyalty to, and show gratitude toward those communities that have enabled her to flourish. But why must this stretch as far as a national community or national institutions? Why is it not sufficient to identify with local and regional and even supranational ones? Why is loyalty to family or church – to kin or *kosmopolis* – not enough? There is no reason in principle why it should not be enough. The nation is not a cultural unit or form of social or political organization that is inscribed in nature's DNA, and no particular nation is guaranteed eternal life. Historically it is surely true, as Benedict Anderson and Linda Colley have argued, that particular nations are human constructs, not natural facts.[7] As they have evolved, so they will change and perhaps pass away. The United Kingdom did not exist before 1707. The United States could have ceased to exist in the early 1860s. Czechoslovakia did cease to exist in 1993.

If historians have reasons to be sceptical of the claims of nations, so do theologians. According to many authoritative students of the phenomenon, the nation as we now know it is a specifically modern entity, appearing first in late eighteenth-century Europe and progressively capitalizing on the cultural decline of the Christian religion. As Europeans lost their faith in God, so the story goes, they transferred their faith to the nation; and as they ceased to hope for life in the world-to-come, they began to invest themselves in the nation's immortality.[8] This certainly seems true of Romantic nationalism, judging by the following statement by Johann Gottlieb Fichte:

> The noble-minded man's belief in the eternal continuance of his influence even on this earth is thus founded on the hope of the eternal continuance of the people from which he has developed, and on the characteristic of that people ... This characteristic is the eternal thing to which he entrusts the eternity of himself and of his continuing influence, the eternal order of things in which he places his portion of eternity... In order to save his nation he must be ready even to die that it may live, and that he may live in it the only life for which he has ever wished.[9]

Given the patently idolatrous character of Romantic nationalism, Karl Barth, writing in the shadow of its infamous Nazi expression, refused to accord the nation any special status at all in the eyes of the one true God. As he presents it in Volume III/4 of his *Church*

---

7   Anderson, B. (1991) *Imagined Communities: Reflections on the Origin and Spread of Nationalism*, rev. ed. London and New York: Verso and Colley, L. (2005) *Britons: Forging the Nation, 1707–1837*. New Haven, CT: Yale University Press.
8   See, for example, Anderson (1991), pp.11–12.
9   Fichte, J.G. (1922) *Addresses to the German Nation*, pp.135–136. Chicago, IL: Open Court Press.

Dogmatics, first published in 1951, national communities, or 'peoples', dissolve into near and far neighbours.[10]

Barth is surely right to puncture the claim of nations of the status of something absolute or essential. Nations are fundamentally constituted by national consciousness, by a sense of national identity, by the feeling of individuals that they belong to this people. And such a sense of community is usually born in reaction against another people, who are culturally different and whose difference grates or threatens: I belong to this people because I oppose that one. Thus the various clans occupying the island of Ireland developed a sense of Irish identity partly in common opposition to English (and Scottish) intrusion. And the English and Scots together developed a sense of British identity partly in common opposition to French Catholic monarchical absolutism and then French revolutionary republicanism. And the various American colonists developed a common sense of American identity first in reaction to the cultural difference of Britons and then in opposition to what they perceived as British tyranny. Since nations are constituted by national consciousness, and since this consciousness is reactive, it follows that nations are contingent in origin.

Notwithstanding this, the fading of the original irritant need not cause the dissolution of common national consciousness, insofar as that consciousness has found institutional expression. For it is through institutions that a people's peculiar linguistic grip on the world, customary incarnation of social values, and political ideals achieve a relatively stable state, which can survive the cooling of the original crucible. These institutions can be cultural and civil social, rather than political; and if political, they can enjoy varying degrees of autonomy. Not every nation is a nation-state; and not every nation-state has maximal sovereignty.

Take Scotland as an example. For almost 300 years from 1707–1999 the Scottish nation expressed its self-consciousness primarily through the Church of Scotland and the Scottish legal system, both of whose jurisdictions covered the same defined territory. While retaining a measure of autonomy over local

---

10   Barth, K. (1961) *Church Dogmatics, 4 vols, Vol. III, 'The Doctrine of Creation', Part 4, 'The Command of God the Creator'*. Edinburgh: T. & T. Clark.

government (much of which operated through the Church or 'Kirk' well into the nineteenth century), the Scots had no autonomous control over economic, welfare, or foreign policy. Insofar as they elected representatives to the British parliament at Westminster, and insofar as their representatives succeeded in wielding influence there, they were able to exercise some control, but it was not autonomous. However, since the devolution of power by the British government to Scotland in 1999, and the recreation of a Scottish parliament, the Scots now exercise a much greater degree of autonomy over the shape of life in the territory of Scotland. Nevertheless, this autonomy is limited: while they can participate in shaping and pursuing a British foreign policy, the Scots still cannot shape and pursue a simply Scottish one. The Scottish nation, therefore, enjoys statehood, but not of a fully sovereign kind.

Nations are contingent, evolving, and transitory phenomena. In that sense, they are artificial, not natural. And they are certainly not divine. However, in another sense they are natural, insofar as their customs and institutions incarnate a particular, perhaps distinctive grasp of the universal forms of flourishing suitable to human nature. Like families and churches and schools and supranational bodies, nations too can embody forms of human good, thus wielding moral authority and obliging our love. Moreover, when nations acquire full statehood, they come to possess maximal power to shape life within their borders so as to defend and promote goods. They also become centres of international agency, which bear responsibility for goods between nation-states, not least that of international order. Insofar as a nation-state has a record of virtuous action internally and externally, shaping life well within and without its borders, it deserves a measure of affection, loyalty, and gratitude as much as any beneficent family or global charity.

BABEL'S BENEFIT: THE GOOD OF A DIVERSITY OF NATIONS

So far I have argued that considered reflection upon the Christian concept of the creatureliness of human being can justify a preference for benefitting near neighbours over distant ones and compatriots over foreigners, that it can also justify affection, loyalty, and gratitude toward those communities, customs, and institutions that mediate forms of human flourishing or human goods, and that a nation is one such community and set of customs and institutions. Now I want to contend that the creaturely quality of the human condition also implies that a diversity of communities, including nations, is a natural necessity that is also good.[11]

Human communities, being creaturely, can only exist in particular times and places; and different geographical locations and historical experiences are bound to generate diverse communities. Human communities, being human, will all share some common characteristics, but experience of different places and histories is bound to generate differences in political constitutions, institutions, customs, received wisdom, and out-look. As a natural necessity, such diversity could be regarded simply as an unhappy feature of the human condition, providing as it does the occasion for inter-communal incomprehension and conflict, and therefore one to be transcended as soon as possible. But Christians, believing as they do in the unqualified goodness and wisdom of the divine Creator, should be disinclined to regard anything natural – whether created or following necessarily from it – as simply evil. Further, human experience confirms that diversity among peoples can be a source of value as well as of conflict. As postmodernists never tire of reminding us, there is beauty in difference. But to restrict this value simply to the aesthetic dimension would be to trivialize many of the differences that concern us here. For differences between constitutions, institutions, customs, wisdom, or outlook, if taken seriously, should provoke reflective engagement, not merely wonder. It should move each community to ask itself whether others do not order their social life better, or whether foreign wisdom should not correct, supplement, or complement its own. The value of communal (and so national) difference here is not just aesthetic, but intellectual and moral: it can enable human beings to learn from each other better ways of serving and promoting the human good. In other words, its justification is not just postmodernist, but liberal (in the style of J.S. Mill).

---

11   See the example of Scotland, given on pages 51–52.

This argument that a Christian vision of things should affirm national diversity is supported by history. According to Adrian Hastings, Christianity has been a vital factor in the historical development of national diversity through its habit of communicating its message by translating it into vernacular languages.[12] Since 'a community...is essentially a creation of human communication',[13] and since the writing down of a language tends to increase linguistic uniformity,[14] the movement of a vernacular from oral usage to the point where it is regularly employed for the production of a literature is a major cause of the development of national identity.[15] Therefore, by translating the Bible into vernacular languages, by developing vernacular liturgies and devotional literature, and by mediating these to the populace through an educated parish clergy, the Christian Church has played a major part in the development of diverse nationalities.[16]

And there is good reason to suppose that this role has not simply been the accidental effect of a particular missionary strategy. After all, different missionary strategies are possible, and we must ask why Christianity chose the one that it did. It could, like Islam, have chosen to spread the Word by assimilation rather than translation. Muslims regard the Qur'an as divine in its Arabic, linguistic form as well as in its content, and the consequent cultural impact of Islam has been to Arabize, 'to draw peoples into a single world community of language and government'.[17] In contrast, Christians do not ascribe divinity to any particular language, and they thereby implicitly recognize that the Word

---

12   Hastings, A. (1997) *The Construction of Nationhood: Ethnicity, Religion, and Nationalism.* Cambridge: Cambridge University Press.
13   Hastings (1997), p.20.
14   Hastings (1997), pp.19–20.
15   Hastings (1997) pp.12, 20, 31.
16   Hastings (1997), pp.22, 24, 191–192. To take one example, the translation of the New Testament into Bulgarian in the mid-nineteenth century was a major factor in crystallising a Bulgarian national identity. According to Mark Mazower (2001), 'Religious changes did more than patriotic activism to shape an emerging Bulgarian consciousness. American Protestant missionaries translated the New Testament into a language Bulgarian peasants could understand, and thereby began to erode the dominance of Greek' (*The Balkans: From the End of Byzantium to the Present Day*, p.99. London: Phoenix Press.
17   Hastings (1997), p.201. This statement needs to be qualified in that the traditional dogma of the untranslateability of the Qur'an has come under question as Islam has established itself in non-Arabic cultures.

of God is free to find (somewhat different) expression in every language.[18] Accordingly, in the New Testament story of the birth of the Christian Church on the day of Pentecost, the disciples of Jesus 'were all filled with the Holy Spirit and began to speak in other tongues', so that the multi-ethnic crowd who heard them 'were bewildered, because each one heard them speaking in his own language' (Acts 2.4, 6). Whereas the story of the tower of Babel in the Hebrew Scriptures presents linguistic diversity as a degeneration (caused by God's punishment of sin) from an original state when 'the whole earth had one language' (Genesis 11.1–9), here the Spirit of God is presented as graciously accommodating Godself to it. This divine self-accommodation implies a respect for, and affirmation of, the historicality, and therefore diversity, of creaturely human being. Such affirmation is also implicit in the orthodox Christian doctrine of the divine Incarnation, according to which God almighty became human in Jesus of Nazareth, and in becoming human became historical – that is, a particular man living in a particular time and place. According to the Christian story, it is characteristic of God to be willing to meet human creatures in the midst of their historicality and diversity. Although transcending time and space, God is not alien to them; in this case what is transcended is not repudiated and may be inhabited. The Christian theological affirmation of human diversity finds further confirmation in the orthodox doctrine of God as a Trinity. In Christian eyes, as in Jewish and Muslim ones, God is certainly one; but the divine unity is not simple. God is more like a community than a monad splendid in isolation. The Origin and Basis of the created world, then, is a unity that contains rather than abolishes difference – a unity in diversity, not instead of it.

In case my affirmation of national diversity should appear idiosyncratic, let me point out that it is a consistent characteristic of Anglican thought from at least the mid-nineteenth century to the present day. So, for example, in 1869 F.D. Maurice affirmed 'the sanctity of national life';[19] distinguished a nation's reverence

---

18 Protestant fundamentalists, who believe the Bible to be inspired by God in the sense of being divinely dictated, come closest among Christians to the traditional Muslim view of the Qur'an; but not even they insist that the Sacred Scriptures should be read publicly only in Hebrew or Greek.

19 Maurice, F.D. (1893) *Social Morality*, p.183. London: Macmillan. These lectures were first published in 1869.

for its own language, laws, and government from a contempt for foreigners;[20] envisaged Christ's kingdom as 'a kingdom for all nations' and not a 'world-empire';[21] and argued that war is lawful only as 'a struggle for Law against Force; for the life of a people as expressed in their laws, their language, their government, against any effort to impose on them a law, a language, a government which is not theirs'.[22] Such views survived the First World War. In his 1928 Henry Scott Holland Memorial Lectures, William Temple affirmed the variety of nations against a non-national cosmopolitanism; and argued that a state has not only the right, but a duty, to defend itself against annihilation, because 'each national community is a trustee for the world-wide community, to which it should bring treasures of its own; and to submit to political annihilation may be to defraud mankind of what it alone could have contributed to the general wealth of human experience'.[23] A little later in his 1935–1936 Gifford Lectures, Hensley Henson drew a sharp distinction between genuine patriotism, which is an extension of neighbourly love, and 'self-centred, vainglorious nationalism': 'Patriotism pictures humanity as a composite of many distinctive national types, enriched with the various achievements of history. Nationalism dreams of a subject world, an empire of its own wherein all men serve its interests and minister to its magnificence'.[24] Most recently, this affirmation of distinctive national life against global imperialism or cosmopolitanism has found expression in the thought of Oliver O'Donovan. In his *The Desire of the Nations: Rediscovering the Roots of Political Theology* (1986), O'Donovan invokes biblical authority in favour of an international order that is unified by universal law rather than by universal, imperial government, and which is constituted by a plurality of nations, each with their own cultural integrity.[25] Unlike empire, 'law holds equal and independent subjects together without allowing one to master the other'.[26]

---

20   Maurice (1893), p.191.
21   Maurice (1893), p.180.
22   Maurice (1893), p.179.
23   Temple, W. (1928) *Christianity and the State, Henry Scott Holland Memorial Lectures 1928*, pp.172, 156. London: Macmillan.
24   Henson, H. (1936) *Christian Morality: Natural, Developing, Final, Gifford Lectures 1935–36*, p.269. Oxford: Clarendon Press.
25   O'Donovan, O. (1986) *The Desire of the Nations: Rediscovering the Roots of Political Theology*, pp.70–73. Cambridge: Cambridge University Press.
26   O'Donovan (1986), p.236.

NATIONAL RESPONSIBILITY TO CREATED NATURAL LAW

Let us pause and review the route taken so far, before we take a further turn. On the biblical ground of an understanding of human being as creaturely, I have argued that it might be preferable to benefit compatriots over foreigners, and that it is justifiable to feel affection, loyalty, and gratitude toward a nation whose customs and institutions have inducted us into created forms of human flourishing. I have also argued on the ground of the doctrines of creation, the Incarnation of God, and the Trinity – as well as by appeal to the consistent witness over more than a century of at least one Christian tradition – that a diversity of nations is a natural phenomenon that generates certain benefits and should be affirmed. That is the rearward view. Now let us turn around again and move forward into different, but complementary, territory, in order to explore the matter of moral responsibility for the common good of all peoples and the limitations this places on national loyalty.

Again, our theological point of departure is the doctrine of creation. As creatures, human beings are bound not only by time and space, but also by the requirements of the good that is proper to their created and universal nature – that is by natural law. Service of the human good is what makes actions right, and failure of such service is what makes them wrong. This good is not just private, but common; the good of the human individual – the good of each human community or nation – is bound up with the good of others, both human and non-human. Acting rightly is important, then, partly because it respects or promotes the good of others in ways they deserve, and partly because in so doing agents maintain or promote their own good – and thereby help to make themselves fit for eternal life.

So human creatures are bound by an obligation to serve the common human good; but being creatures, their powers of service are limited. No human effort, individual or collective, has the power to secure the maximal good of all human beings (including the dead as well as the living), far less of non-human ones as well. Each of us must choose to do what he can, and what he may, to advance certain dimensions of the good of some, trusting divine

Providence to coordinate all our little contributions and guide their unpredictable effects to the benefit of the common good. Among those whom we choose to help, it would be right for us to include our benefactors, for gratitude requires it. This is the justification for special loyalties to such communities as one's family and nation.

But note: what one owes one's family or nation is not anything or everything, but specifically respect for and promotion of their good. Such loyalty, therefore, does not involve simply doing or giving whatever is demanded, whether by the state, the electoral majority, or even the people as a whole. Indeed, when what is demanded would appear to harm the community – for example, acquiescence in injustice perpetrated by the state against its own people or a foreign one, or by one section of the nation against another – genuine national loyalty requires that it be refused. True patriotism is not uncritical – as the fierce criticism of the Jews' own ruling classes by the Old Testament's prophets and by Jesus himself should make clear. And in extreme circumstances true patriotism might even involve participation in acts of treason – as it did in the case of Dietrich Bonhoeffer, whose love for Germany led him into conspiracy to kill Hitler.[27] National loyalty, as Christians should conceive it, shows itself basically in reminding the nation that it is accountable to God, at least in the sense of being obliged by the good given or created in human nature. By thus distinguishing between its object and God, such loyalty distances itself from the Romantic nationalism that absolutizes and divinizes the 'Nation', making its unquestioning service the route to a quasi-immortality.

It is true, of course, that the Christian Bible contains and gives prominence to the concept of a People chosen by God to be the medium of salvation to the world; and it is also true that particular Christianized nations have periodically identified themselves as the Chosen People, thereby pretending to accrue to themselves and their imperial, putatively civilizing, policies an exclusive divine authority. But, as I have already pointed out, the notion of the Chosen People as referring to a particular nation strictly belongs to the Old Testament, not the New; and

---

27   For a fuller exploration of these themes in the light of Bonhoeffer's life and work, see Clements, K. (1986) *True Patriotism: Love of Country in Dialogue with the Witness of Dietrich Bonhoeffer*. London: Collins.

one of the main points on which early Christianity differentiated itself from Judaism was precisely its transnational character. Full participation in the Christian religion was no longer tied to worship in the Temple at Jerusalem, and was as open to Gentiles as to Jews; for, as Paul famously put it, 'there is neither Jew nor Greek, ...; for you are all one in Christ Jesus' (Galatians 3.28). In early, emergent Christianity, the 'People of God' came to refer, no longer to a particular nation (Israel), but to the universal Church. Certainly, there have been many times when the Church as an institution has become wedded to a particular ethnic culture or the instrument of a particular nation-state. There have been times when the Church's affirmation of a particular culture or nation has become unconditional. Nevertheless, in the light of what we have said above, we may judge that these are times when the Church has betrayed its identity and failed in its calling. They are times when it has failed to maintain the distinction ironically attested by the Nazi judge, who, before condemning Helmuth James von Moltke to death, demanded of him, 'From whom do you take your orders? From the Beyond or from Adolf Hitler?'[28] and they are times when it has failed to observe the original priority so succinctly affirmed in Sir Thomas More's declaration, moments before he was beheaded for refusing to endorse Henry VIII's assertion of royal supremacy over the English Church, that he would die 'the King's good servant, but God's first'.[29]

A properly Christian view, then, insists that every nation is equally accountable to God for its service of the human good. No nation may pretend to be God's Chosen People in the strong sense of being the sole and permanent representative and agent of His will on earth; no nation may claim such an identity with God. This relativization still permits each nation to consider itself chosen or called by God to contribute in its own peculiar way to the world's salvation, to play a special role – at once unique,

---

28   von Moltke, H.J. (1991) *Letters to Freya: A Witness against Hitler*, p.409. London: Collins Harvill.

29   According to a contemporary report carried in the *Paris News Letter*. See Harpsfield, N. (1932) *The Life and Death of Sir Thomas Moore, Knight, Sometymes Lord High Chancellor of England*. E.V. Hitchcock and R.W. Chambers (eds), Early English Text Society, Original Series no. 186. London: Oxford University Press, Appendix III, p.266: 'Apres les exhorta, et supplia tres instamment qu'ils priassent Dieu pour le Roy, affin qu'il luy voulsist donner bon conseil, protestant qu'il mouroit son bon serviteur et de Dieu premierement'.

essential, and limited – in promoting the universal human good. It allows members of a given nation to celebrate the achievements of the good that grace their own history and to take pride in the peculiar institutions and customs in which they have realized it. At the same time, it forces them to acknowledge that their nation's achievement is but one among many, and so to recognize, appreciate, and even learn from the distinctive contributions of others.

But more than this, each nation must realize not only that other nations too have made valuable contributions to the realization of the common good of all things, but also that the achievement of the good in one nation is actually bound up with its achievement elsewhere. National loyalty, therefore, is properly extrovert. As Karl Barth put it:

> when we speak of home, motherland, and people, it is a matter of outlook, background, and origin. We thus refer to the initiation and beginning of a movement. It is a matter of being faithful to this beginning. But this is possible only if we execute the movement, and not as we make the place where we begin it a prison and stronghold. The movement leads us relentlessly, however, from the narrower sphere to a wider, from our own people to other human peoples... The one who is really in his own people, among those near to him, is always on the way to those more distant, to other peoples.[30]

The point here is not that we should grow out of national identity and loyalty and into a cosmopolitanism that, floating free of all particular attachments, lacks any real ones;[31] but rather that, in and through an ever-deepening care for the good of our own nation, we are drawn into caring for the good of foreigners. This point is poignantly captured by Yevgeni Yevtushenko in 'Babii Yar', his poem about Russian anti-Semitism:

---

30   Barth (1961), pp.293–294.
31   Barth is right to suggest that such cosmopolitanism is not only undesirable, but impossible: 'The command of God certainly does not require any man to be a cosmopolitan, quite apart from the fact that none of us can really manage to be so' (1961, p.293). Here I differ from Richard Miller (2001, pp.27–28), who understands Barth's 'overall impetus' to be 'universalist', and interprets him as granting national identity and loyalty only 'provisional' affirmation.

Oh my Russian people!
I know you are internationalists to the core.
But those with unclean hands
have often made a jingle of your purest name.
I know the goodness of my land ....
In my blood there is no Jewish blood.
In their callous rage all anti-semites
must hate me now as a Jew.
For that reason I am a true Russian.[32]

Notwithstanding the tensions that may arise between national loyalty and more extensive ones, there is nevertheless an essential connection between them.

CONCLUSION

In this chapter, I have argued that Christianity, making sense of the various views in the Bible, at once affirms patriotism and qualifies it. Nation-states are natural, insofar as they incarnate universal human goods in their customs and institutions. And since it is natural and right for human beings to love those goods and to be grateful to those communities that make them present, it is also right that citizens should be patriotic. Nevertheless, nation-states are not divine; they are human constructs, which rise and fall, come and go. What is more, they can sin and sin greatly. Therefore, genuine patriotism sometimes requires Christians to offer loyal opposition.

---

32 Yevtushenko, Y. (1991) 'Babii Yar.' In *The Collected Poems, 1952–90*, pp.103–104. Edinburgh: Mainstream Publishing. 'Babii Yar' is the name of a ravine on the outskirts of Kiev where at least 100,000 Jews were massacred in 1941. The massacre was carried out by German troops; but not without the tacit approval of many local Ukrainians, who shared in the long Russian tradition of anti-Semitism.

Chapter Three

SOCIAL HARMONY IN THE MIDDLE EAST
The Christian Contributions

Najib George Awad, Connecticut, USA

THE LIFE-OR-DEATH INQUIRY

Since 2010, the Arab part of the Middle East has been inflicted with a dire situation of turmoil, instability, violence, clashes and socio-political and sectarian divisiveness that radically damaged the entire existence and threatened the fate of all ethnicities, religions and confessional segments in the region. This radical, insufferable transformation manifested itself in diverse forms during the past few years: in a form of public demonstrations known as the 'Arab Spring' (i.e. in Tunisia, Egypt, Morocco, Saudi Arabia), in a form of public riots and regime collapse (i.e. in Libya and Yemen) or, more drastically and tragically, in the form of bloody, devastatingly nihilistic war(s), like the tragedy that is currently tearing Syria apart. While the people of Syria are right now fully entangled with sheer survival, hoping to just have a 'tomorrow' in the midst of the dark waters they strive to swim through, Syrian intellectuals and activists occupy themselves with crucial conjectures about post-war Syria and post-Arab Spring Middle East. One of these questions they ponder sharply is related to the nature and features of the Syrian and Arab societal contexts and civil public squares that will rise from the ashes of the present dark times: would we still be able to recognize possible, peaceful, harmonious, tolerant, pluralist, multi-religious, multi-confessional, multi-ethnic and multi-cultural Arab/Middle Eastern (Syria included) societies in that part of the world, as one, at least figuratively, used to encounter in that region before 2010?

As a constitutive component of the human textile of the Middle East – Eastern, Arab and non-Arab – Christians find themselves suffering with their non-Christian compatriots and instinctively striving to survive the lethal havoc that wrecks their homeland. They are also haunted by the same life-or-death question of the future of their existence in Syria: would Christians in Syria and the Middle East still find a socially and publicly harmonious and tolerant life-setting, wherein they can safely, peacefully, communally and religiously exist as citizens equal to the members of other predominantly Muslim groups? And, if this is still possible, what role can, or even should, these Christians play to contribute to the recreation of such a social harmony?

CHRISTIANS IN THE MIDDLE EAST: A HISTORY OF SUFFERING AND SECURITY

Before 2010, foreign visitors to the region used to hold particular views about the Christians' condition in the context of the Muslim-majority societies of the Arab World. These views tended often to be sentimental, or even euphoric, in nature and were mostly the results of the excitement of travellers who regularly visited the Near East and left it fascinated with the stunning array of the architectural beauty of the stratified and intermingling churches and mosques in almost every city therein.[1]

The fascination of the historical multi-religious presence and co-existence in the Middle East notwithstanding, perceiving in depth the real situation of the Christians in the Arab World needs to be pursued vis-à-vis existing, down-to-earth aspects other than the above mentioned touristic one.

The external rich history of plurality that is portrayed via the architectural versatility hides underneath it an internal, parallel [double-faced, almost paradoxical] history of suffering [and peacefulness], certainty [and confidence], fear [and security],

---

1   See Awad, N.G. (2012a) *And Freedom Became a Public-Square: Political, Sociological and Religious Overview on the Arab Christians and the Arabic Spring*, pp.59–67. Berlin and Zürich: LIT Verlag.

See also Kerr, D.A. (2003) 'A Western Christian Appreciation of the Eastern Christianity.' In B.J. Bailey and J.M. Bailey (eds) *Who Are the Christians in the Middle East?*, pp.3–11. Grand Rapids, MI/Cambridge, UK: Eerdmans.

pressure [and comfort], difficulties [and progress], death [and survival].[2]

The Eastern Christians' history is a multifarious, sophisticated narrative of 'perpetual strife for survival as a minority in a non-Christian majority world'.[3] It is actually the fact that even before the latest catastrophic changes in the region, 'the scale of the Christians' decline is indelibly high on the demographic, sociological and cultural scales, as a fast look at the radical drop-down of the Christians' percentage in the region's countries during the past forty years clearly shows'.[4] During the past five years (since 2011), nonetheless, the Christians' situation has even radically worsened due to the Sunnite–Shi'ite violent clash – which has been ignited again due to the regional power struggle between Iran and Saudi Arabia – and in the Syrian and Iraqi territories, the mushrooming of fanatic, terrorist Islamic entities like ISIS, Jabhat an-Nusra, Hizbullah, Jaysh al-Fath, Jaysh al-Islam, Kata'ib al-Jaysh al-Sha'bi, etc.

Nothing is comparably more relevant to the question of the Christians' role in the future of the Middle East than the Syrian Christians' stance and role in relation to the tragic situation and destructive war that continues to demolish the heart of the Near East, Syria. Today, no question on the fate and future of Christians in the Middle East can be accurately and plausibly answered without discerning the situation of Christians in that heart of the region called the Syrian territories.

CHRISTIANS AND THE SYRIAN TRAGEDY

Scholars and observers have witnessed for a long time the radical decrease of the number of Christians in the Middle East. Due to diverse factors and circumstances, Christians started to emigrate in large numbers from the region toward the Western world starting in the late 1970s.[5] Eastern Christians' emigration from

2   Awad (2012a), p.60.
3   Awad (2012a), p.60.
4   Awad (2012a), p.62.
5   This was not the only immigration wave in the twentieth century; various other waves had occurred in the previous decades of that century. But it was probably the largest-scale migration the Christians made before the five years from 2011 to the time of writing.

their homeland reached a critical climax in the first decade of the twenty-first century. Due to the first and second Gulf Wars in Iraq, tens of thousands of Iraqi Christians escaped from their lands and found their way to Europe, the UK and the USA. Most recently, starting specifically from 2012 until now, and in the light of the destruction of almost 80 per cent of their homeland, over one-and-a-half million Syrian Christians (including my own brother) were displaced and forced to take the journey of death from Syria, via Turkey, across the sea to Greece to reach refuge in Europe. Out of the two million Christians who were part of Syria's 22 million inhabitants, hardly 500,000 (including the rest of my family) are still trapped in between the fighting factions inside the Syrian battleground and sheltering in the coastal territories of Western Syria, the last semi-battle-free zone in the country. They remain there because they could not find a way out of the country to any expatriate haven. This drastic, and seemingly non-stoppable, drainage and displacement of Syrian, and Eastern, Christians in the Middle East makes us share Jean-Pierre Valognes' factual concern and state with him:

> Will there still be any Christians in the East in the third millennium? Although they are unlikely to disappear altogether... one can still reasonably believe that they will be reduced to a few individuals anonymously dispersed and no longer able to maintain the communal life which is vital for preserving a specific identity. Once their numbers became too scarce for them to make any impact, the only option left to them will be that of modelling themselves on the prevailing values. They will then no longer recognize themselves as Christians. This means that what constituted their richness will be lost.[6]

Valognes' tenable alarm applies to Christians nowhere else today as much as to those in Syria. Syrian Christians not only face the question of their survival and longevity in their homeland. They are also inescapably confronted with the question of whether Syria can remain in the future a life-setting that allows them to

---

6   Valognes, J.P. (1994) *Vie et mort des Chrétiens d'Orient*. Paris: Foyard. p.18; as cited in O'Mahoney, A. (2009) 'Christianity in Iraq: Modern History, Theology, Dialogue and Politics (Until 2003),' in E.C.D. Hunter (ed.) *The Christian Heritage of Iraq: Collected Papers from the Christianity of Iraq, I–V Seminar Days*. Piscataway, NJ: Georgias Press, pp.237–284.

live, and contribute to the lives of others, in their homeland as 'Christians', as truly 'Christ-like' followers of particular values, or whether Syria's situation would, rather, prevent them from maintaining their richness and particularity as 'Christians'. Would their presence in their homeland be at the expense of compromising their particular identity?

It is with the sadness of a patriotic Christian from Syria that I state my answer to the above question in the following words: the latest developments in the situation in Syria and the devastating consequences of the war suggest that there does not seem to be any horizon left for the Christians' presence in Syria, at least not in the foreseeable future.[7] I do realize that my answer sounds pessimistic and controversial to the ears of other Syrian and Arab Christians who are still inside the region striving to survive and even dreaming of remaining for the rest of their lives in Syria, whatever it is eventually transformed into. I am a theologian and a Christian–Muslim Relations scholar. Politically and culturally, I am secularist–liberal, and I refuse to view people from the narrow perspective of their confession, religion or their doctrinal or dogmatic convictions. This narrowly categorizing view is far from my principles and ethical beliefs. As I endeavour in the ensuing paragraphs to elaborate on my answer to the above question, I pursue this goal primarily as a Syrian citizen from the Syrian Christian community who profoundly and seriously thinks about the forthcoming ramifications of Syria's present situation.

First of all, I conceptually differentiate between 'presence' and 'existence' in my reflection on Christians' contribution to the human life and social harmony in the Middle East. 'Existence' connotes the spatio-temporal and physical subsistence in a particular state, land or territorial boundaries that are defined by means of geography, national-state borders and national-human communal entity-formation. On the contrary, 'presence' designates the particular characteristics of the role, influence,

---

7   The ensuing paragraphs after this point are derived from Awad, N.G. (2016) 'Lā Ufuq ll-Ḥuḍūr al-Masīḥī fī Sūriyyā' (No Horizon to the Christian Presence in Syria). *Al-'Arabī al-Ǧadīd Newspaper*, 6 February. Available at https://www.alaraby.co.uk/opinion/2016/2/6/%D9%84%D8%A7-%D8%A3%D9%81%D9%82-%D9%84%D9%84%D8%AD%D8%B6%D9%88%D8%B1-%D8%A7%D9%84%D9%85%D8%B3%D9%8A%D8%AD%D9%8A-%D9%81%D9%8A-%D8%B3%D9%88%D8%B1%D9%8A%D8%A9, accessed on 2 May 2017.

contribution and signifying features of specific societal and communal segments of people that are part of the spatio-temporal and physical existence of the broader human public which exists in this particular territory. In this essay, my attention is not directed toward the Christians' existence in Syria: there will probably always be Christians, few or not, existing in that part of the world, and they will be called 'Syrians' or 'Eastern Christians' in the Middle East. My focus is rather directed to the Christians' 'presence' therein. I focus, that is, on their potential role, impact, influence and unique contribution to the human life in that geographical territory. What I am suggesting is that, though they exist, and will probably exist still, in Syria, the Christians' presence therein does not seem likely to result in a role and impact wherein these Christians can effectively contribute to the social harmony in the future Syria (or even the Middle East) by means of their definition as Christians and nothing else. The situation of their existence in the Middle East (and Syria in particular) suggests to me that the Christians' presence and role will not be allowed to portray a unique identity that is shaped after particular Christian values and Christ-like principles. I construct my assessment upon the following two contextual factors.

First, Eastern Christians, Syrians included, have always opted historically for defining themselves by virtue of a confirmed affiliation to the sociological, cultural and historical human existence of the states they belong to and live in as citizens, regardless of these states' religious or non-religious identity. In regard to this particular point, the Christians of Syria were unique: they have never dreamt of establishing their own, distinct state-like entity. They have chosen instead to become the 'godfathers' of the choice of creating and belonging to a conclusive, collectivist, either 'Syrian' or 'Arab', unifying identity and to define themselves by means of it. In the light of today's condition of the Syrian public, in the midst of the tragic disaster that inflicts the country, any existing unifying national identity (i.e. 'Syrian' or 'Arab') has started to lose ground and almost vanish from the self-awareness and self-understanding consciousness of the Syrian public: many Syrians hardly define themselves today as 'Syrians' or as 'Arab-Syrians'. The Syrian nation has recently disintegrated into confessional, ethnic, religious and demographic, even locational, small entities, and its members narrowly define themselves by means of a sharp 'self-othering' presumption. As I already stated, the Christians of Syria predominantly opted for belonging to a unifying 'Syrian' or 'Arab' national identity, not to a divisive confessional, ethnic or religious one. Therefore, any considerable, factual 'presence' for them will not be realistically tenable in the context of a forthcoming Syria that inevitably portrays a rapid drift into becoming a society and state shaped after confessional boundaries, religious borders, ethnic particularities and a demographic allotting mentality.

Second, if Syrian Christians were asked about the role and presence they imagine themselves engaging with in Syria's future, a predominant part of them would relate that such a 'presence' depends on the possible establishment of a factual pluralist and inclusive state and the principles and constituting presumptions upon which this state will be created. Christians in Syria in particular, and the Middle East in general, have often articulated the conviction that what would grant them a dignified life of law-rule justice and true civil citizenship, and what will maintain their natural human rights and treat them as equal citizens, is none other than a politically, constitutionally and culturally (not necessarily socially) secular system that is based on the principle of civil citizenship and positivist, pluralist and democratic legislative and constitutional foundations.[8] They believe in a system that does not treat them as sects, reduce them to a mere confessional congregation, deem them followers of a minority-religious belief, alienate them as members of a foreign ethnicity or even trap them one more time in an old Dhimmi situation, where they are seen as

---

8   On the possibility of secularism in the Arab World, see Awad (2012a), pp.19–39 and Awad, N.G. (2015a) 'Muğtamaʿāt Madaniyya Muʾlmanah: Ahūa Mumkin am Ḥulm ʿAṣṣī ʿan at-Taḥqīq?' (Secularized Civil Societies: Is it Possible or Impossible?) Al-Ğadīd Magazine, 12 January. Available at www.aljadeedmagazine.com/?id=1138, accessed on 21 March 2017. On secularity and its relation to the understanding of 'Civil' in the political mind of the Syrian Muslim Brothers, see Awad, N.G. (2014a) 'Is secularity by any means imaginable? A reading of the idea of "civil state" in the Syrian Muslim Brotherhood's contemporary political project for the Syria of the future.' Islamochristiana 40, 105–124 and Taylor, C. (2007) A Secular Age. Cambridge, MA: Harvard University Press.

Taylor, C. (2009) 'Foreword: What is Secularism?' In G.B. Levey and T. Modood (eds) Secularism, Religion and Multicultural Citizenship, pp.xi–xxii. Cambridge and New York: Cambridge University Press.

a minority in need of protection, tolerance and benevolence from the majority.

The observer of the recently boiling Middle East and burning Syria cannot but concede that Syria, or any Middle Eastern country for that matter, is not going in the near future to be re-established in such a civil, pluralist, inclusive, secular identity. One cannot but realize that there seems to be a local-Syrian and regional-Middle Eastern, but also international, decision-making tendency to impose on the future Syria a ruling system, wherein people's share in power and decision-making is decided and granted in accordance with their religious, sectarian and numerical presence, not according to their equal civil citizenship. In the midst of this context, the Christians of Syria will mostly fail to be effective players or participants in such a socio-political structure. They will fail to be partnering players in it not just because they are not experienced and skilled in following such a system's rules and expectations, but also because it is not the ultimate choice or the imagining of their dominant majority. The predominant stance of rejecting violence and war and parting ways with its clashing sides, the regime and its opposition alike, which the Christian public (though not the church prelates, as I will demonstrate further down) has been clinging to since the beginning of the revolution in Syria,[9] frankly demonstrates before us that Christians do not picture themselves involved in any role or embodying any presence that will make them part of such a divisive system like the one described above.

In the light of the two factors discussed above, I conclude that the present Syrian scene defies any potential presence or role to the Christians in the near future of Syria. The Christians of Syria have always predominantly agreed to be part of a 'nation', not to create their own self-existing, religiously defined nation. The question of their role in maintaining such a unified nation's social harmony is, therefore, greatly significant. The answer to such a serious challenge, nevertheless, does not seem to be positive or encouraging in the light of the recently available data. One has

---

9   See Awad, N.G. (2013a) 'The Christians and the Syrian Revolution: Which Fears from the Rebellion? Which Political System in the Future?' In M. Raheb (ed.) *The Arabic Spring and the Christians of the Middle East*, pp.113–127. Bethlehem: Diyar Publishers.

to add here that part of the responsibility for the lack of any possible role for the Christians in the future of Syrian society is actually, and unfortunately, the responsibility of these Christians' leaders and church representatives. It is not just something for which these Christians can blame the region's non-Christians.

THE FALLEN-NESS OF THE ECCLESIAL PRELATES

In the previous section, I endeavoured to demonstrate that, while Christians in the Middle East in general, and in Syria in particular, may not relinquish their existence in the region in the future, these Christians would probably lack any tangible presence or influential role in the future societal and state recreation of the Syrian nation. In this section, I attempt to demonstrate that the Syrian (and Middle Eastern) Christians themselves are considerably responsible for this lack of presence and role in the scene of their homeland. It is not always the case that these Christians are victims of non-Christians' prevalence and influence. It is not always the case that they are victimized because of their sheer religious, non-Islamic otherness. The Christians of Syria (and the Middle East) are partially the culprits of their own fecklessness and lack of resources. The primary culprits among the Christian public, who put them in this useless, helpless and feckless situation, as I will explain, are the church servants and ecclesial prelates from all the Syrian Christian denominations.[10]

Syrian Christians know in their hearts, and usually complain to one another, that, during the past five decades, the highest ranks of their spiritual and clerical prelates have colluded with the al-Assad (senior and junior) tyrannical regime in a multi-faceted relational network of allegiance, subordination, opportunism, mutual interest and self-seeking. The Christian public expresses its dissent of such a pragmatic alliance, because it believes that it did not serve the broader Christian community and its life, but it was rather developed at the expense of this community's credibility

---

10   The ensuing paragraphs are inspired by an article that was published for me in French. See Awad, N.G. (2013b) 'Il faut sauver les chrétiens de Syrie, mais de quoi?' *Le Monde*, 17 September. Available at www.lemonde.fr/idees/article/2013/09/17/il-faut-sauver-les-chretiens-de-syrie-mais-de-quoi_3479209_3232.html, accessed on 21 March 2017.

and relation to the rest of the Syrian public. Since the breaking out of the Syrian public revolution (which started as purely peaceful, civil demonstrations),[11] these clerical partners and allies of the regime started to systematically propagate before the local and international media and the international idea-creating and decision-making circles that the entire Eastern Christian congregation could not foresee any salvation and existence in the Middle East if the al-Assad regime collapsed. In past years, some of these clerics even habituated eulogizing the dictator, al-Assad, from the pulpits and press venues and claimed him as the 'Messianic' godfather of Christians and praised his rule as providing the Christians' promised kingdom of safety and security. The purpose of their false statements was to emphasize an imaginary, unprecedented idealist state of existing in the shadow of al-Assad's regime, as if the Arab-Eastern Christians, not just in Syria but in the region, did not really enjoy any safe, peaceful and prosperous existence at all before this regime and would have none after its departure.

On the other hand, these prelates transmitted in their discourse before the Western church and public opinion the most negative, demonizing and distorting propaganda against the civil demonstrations and the public rebellion in the country. They falsely reduced the Syrian revolution into a mere religious hatred conflict, as they perpetually alleged that these demonstrators and rebels were blindly driven by their religious fanatic hatred towards every non-Muslim segment of Syrian society. They affirmed that this revolution was a dire threat to the Christian existence (a 'religious persecution' myth) and it was directed against them primarily (as if the Christians of the region had never co-existed with Muslims in that land for over 1,400 years).

---

11   On the transformation of the revolution into wars, see Awad, N.G. (2012b) 'Man Ḥaūwala al-Ṭaūrah as-Sūriyya ilā Sāḥat Ma'rakah wa-Limāḏā?' (Who Transformed the Syrian Revolution into a Battle-Zone and Why?) *al-Aūwān*, 27 November. Available at http://bit.ly/2qAAEuG, accessed on 6 March 2016; Awad, N.G. (2012c) 'Ī'ādat Qirā'a ll-Ḥārīṭah: Man ma' Māḏā wa li-Māḏā?' (Re-Reading the Map: Who with What and Why?) *al-Mustaqbal Newpaper*, 24 June. Available at www.almustaqbal. com/v4/Article.aspx?Type=np&Articleid=527429, accessed on 21 March 2017; and Awad, N.G. (2015b) 'Kaī Lā Nūwaṣṣif Ḥaṭa'an mā Yaḥuṭ wa Limāḏā Ḥadaṭa fī Sūrīyyā!!' (Lest We Misread What Happens and Why Did it Happen in Syria!!) *al-Mustaqbal Newspaper*, 19 April. Available at www.almustaqbal.com/v4/Article. aspx?Type=NP&ArticleID=657817, accessed on 21 March 2017.

Be that as it may, and driven by its belief in the propagandist discourse of these Christian prelates, the international church and lay public circles opted ever since for similarly approaching the Syrian public opposition to the al-Assad regime with a high level of suspicion and scepticism, revealing serious hesitation to back up any political or diplomatic (though not humanitarian) support of the Syrian public dream of freedom, democracy, justice and regime-change (which the Christian public also shares).

The role which the Christian Syrian prelates played in the service of the tyrannical regime, especially in the service of proliferating the premeditated demonization of Muslims and victimization of Christians in the country, had a direly damaging impact on the Christian public's image in Syrian society: it made them lose the majority of their Muslim co-citizens' solidarity and acceptance, as their credibility and national adherence to Syrian public rights has now been marred with accusations of betrayal, disloyalty and self-favouritism. In their unfair and fishy defilement of the Syrian public's uprising against the tyrannical dictatorship, these clerical prelates dug a huge gap between the Christians and their broader, Muslim societal life-setting in Syria in a manner that deprived the Christians of any credible, trustworthy mediating role they could have been able to play in healing the country, bringing the fighting factions into reconciliation and paving the way for the restoration of harmony and cohesion between societal segments in any future Syria.

According to Christian faith as it exists in the Bible, Christians are commanded by their Messiah to be messengers of peace, reconciliation and forgiveness in their living contexts. Syrian Christians are now deprived of practising this mission because of their religious leaders' bias and inequity. Yes, the Christians need salvaging in the Middle East. However, the salvation they need is from the dangerous consequences of the tendentious actions of those among them who allowed the ruling corrupted powers to exploit them as mere instruments in the service of these corrupted rulers' biased obsessions with survival, profit and favouritism. Syrian Christians will never be invited to play any role or allowed to enjoy any effective presence in Syrian society unless they are rescued from the polarizing and self-alienating stance of the circle of the regime's agents among their ecclesial prelates. They need to be urgently rescued from the latter's catastrophic decision of always stretching an arm of loyalty and submission to the power- and authority-holder, instead of opening two arms of friendship and partnership towards the broader Syrian public, embracing this public's choices and advocating for the oppressed, persecuted and tyrannized amongst them. The difference between this latter choice or the choice of succumbing to a polarizing personal self-interest and self-survival marks sharply, in fact, the substantial difference between being nominally 'Christian' and being genuinely and actually 'Christ-like'.

THE CHRISTIANS' CONTRIBUTIONS:
A FEW THEOLOGICAL–BIBLICAL INSIGHTS

Achieving social harmony in a multi-religious, multi-ethnic, multi-confessional, multi-cultural and multi-denominational context like the Middle East is a dauntingly challenging task indeed. It has always been so, and it is probably going to remain so in the foreseeable future, especially in the light of the multifarious and self-breeding violence, war and conflicts in the region. In the midst of such a situation, one cannot imagine any possible and sustainable social cohesion, communal unity and co-existence without first and foremost extinguishing violence by means of peace. Peace (in its broader societal and humanitarian senses, not just in the senses of 'ceasefire' or 'no-war' situations) becomes the backbone of any potential social harmony in this case, because peace carries within its nature the same foundational notion of 'relationship' that is inherent to any form of sociality. 'Peace is the reflection of people's relationships with each other. It is not how people think about themselves and the different others before them. It is basically how people relate to others and act before them and over against them in daily-life and realistic contexts.'[12]

If Middle Eastern Christians would have a tangible presence and influential impact on social harmony in Syria in particular, and the Arab World in general, becoming peacemakers and mediators of peace and reconciliation is their inescapable passage, if not the only valuable 'Christ-like' one, to achieve this goal. Middle Eastern

---

12   Awad (2012a), p.188.

Christians, more than any other community, can play the role of 'the mediator' who facilitates a resolution to the clash between the Muslim (Sunnite vs. Shi'ite) struggling factions. Peacemaking and peace-mediating are genuine expressions of the Christian biblical message, as the idea of 'peace' is a recurring theme in the Christian Scripture: peace is one of the fruits of the Holy Spirit ('the fruits of the Spirit are love, joy, peace, patience, kindness, generosity, faithfulness, gentleness and self-control' (Galatians 5.22)); those who tend to achieve peace are praised by Christ ('blessed are the peacemakers, for they will be called children of God' (Matthew 5.9)); peace is one of the divine promises which God bestows upon His people ('and I will give peace in the land, and ye shall lie down, and none shall make you afraid, and I will rid evil beasts out of the land, neither shall the sword go through your land' (Leviticus 26.6)); finally, God's view of human existence is shaped after peace and not victory or material prosperity ('for the kingdom of God is not meat and drink; but righteousness and peace and joy in the Holy Spirit' (Romans 14.17)).[13] Be that as it may, when it comes to Christians' contribution to social harmony in the context of the Middle East, one has to find some plausible theological and biblical answers to the following question: 'how can Arab/Middle Eastern Christians [in Syria and other states] be a vehicle of peace in such a prone-to-violence, [polarizingly] versatile and [challengingly] complex [social] context as the Middle East?'[14]

I have already addressed such a question and tendered a possible response elsewhere.[15] I will not, thus, repeat my reflection on it here. What I will pursue is just pointing to what I believe is going to deprive the Christians of the Middle East of playing any peacekeeping or peace-mediating role that could be needed to recreate possible social harmony in their broader, predominantly Muslim-Arab societies. My theological–biblical proposal is the following: Christians may not be permitted to act

---

13 For some literature on peace in Christianity, see, for example, Miller, M.E. and Gengrich, B.N. (eds) (1994) *The Church's Peace Witness*. Cambridge, MA: Eerdmans; Yoder, J.H. (2009) *Christian Attitudes to War, Peace and Revolution*. Grand Rapids, MI: Brazos Press; and Lang, M.G. (ed.) (2011) *Christian Peace and Nonviolence: A Documentary History*. Maryknoll, NY: Orbis Books.
14 Awad (2012a), p.189.
15 Awad (2012a), pp.186–204.

as peacemakers in their societies because, due to the actions of their church prelates, their surrounding context does not seem any more ready to believe that Christians maintain the most central requirement for conflict resolution, namely neutrality and impartiality. By sacrificing impartiality in the service of self-survival and self-interest, the Christian ecclesial prelates threw themselves and the Christian public with them into the lap of the dictatorial, tyrannical authority-holders, creating, eventually, the impression in society that Christians decided to break away from the broader civil public and relinquish its search for freedom, justice, democracy, human dignity and natural basic human rights. By such polarizing behaviour, these prelates not only turned Christians into *personae non gratae* in the eyes of their Muslim compatriots. They also alienated the Christian community from its very own 'Christ-like' faith, which lies in Jesus' teaching 'you will know the truth, and the truth will set you free' (John 8.32).

Back in the ninth century, when the Middle Eastern Christians were living in the shadow of the Muslim–Abbasid Caliphate in their homeland (as the extant chronicles of the fourteenth-century Syriac prelate, St Michael the Great, record for us), the Jacobite–Monophysite patriarch, Dionysius of Tell Maḥrē, stood face-to-face with the Muslim caliph, al-Mā'mūn. With the admirably bold frankness of someone serving 'the truth', the patriarch defied the Muslim ruling authority's violent suppression of Coptic rebels, who demonstrated on the streets of Cairo against the Muslim governor of Egypt. The Christian prelate daringly related to the caliph that the root of the rebellion was the corruption of the governor and his oppression and discrimination against societal segments in the country. The Christian prelate did not even shy away from or fear 'reminding [the caliph] of the account that he would give before God concerning the flock that had been entrusted to him'.[16] In his courageous obedience to Jesus' teaching in John 8.32, patriarch Dionysius in the ninth century

---

16   Harrak, A. (2015) 'Dionysius of Tell-Maḥrē: Patriarch, Diplomat and an Inquisitive Chronicler'. In M. Doerffer, E. Fiano and K. Smith (eds) *Syriac Encounters: Papers from the Sixth North American Syriac Symposium*, pp.215–235, p.222. Leuven: Peeters. The chronicle then relates 'the caliph, who listened attentively to the patriarch, said: "these *'ummāl*-agents do not act according to my will. I do not intend to burden people, and if I have mercy on the Romans who are my enemies, how could I fail to be merciful toward my flock? If God wills, I will straighten up everything"'.

was advocating and vouching for the state-rights of his co-citizens as someone incarnating Jesus' ministry in factual social actions. He is one of these Christians from the past history of the Middle East, who exemplify before us a Christ-follower standing before kings and governors (Matthew 10.18) to advocate for truth and justice. Quite contrary is this prophetic example from the past to the stances of church leaders in today's Middle East (especially Syria) before the ruling regimes of their countries.

In their support at all costs of the ruling, tyrannical and corrupted regime (i.e. Syria), as well as their involvement in the sectarian clash for power and monopolization by all (mostly destructive) means (e.g. Lebanon), Christians seem to be betraying Jesus' teaching to 'give back to Caesar what is Caesar's and to God what is God's' (Mark 12.17). They rather image what can be deemed a drifting into a counter-biblical (if not even 'anti-biblical') trap, which Christians unfortunately have fallen into more than once before throughout their long, Eastern and Western, history. Abraham van De Beek eloquently describes this trap when he calls it a Christian expression of 'merging politics and religion' in such a manner that is reminiscent of earliest Christianity's conflation of Christian faith with the Roman empire; when that is, a Christian church father like Eusebius of Caesarea, for example, paved the way for such a dangerous merging by deeming the lay leader (emperor) a representative of the kingship of Christ.[17]

A similar merging of political self-protectionism and Christian identity seems to be clearly taking place in Middle Eastern Christians' lives today. The Christian clerical and lay leaders therein not only reflect indifference to Christ's 'Caesar's-vs.-God's' equation. They also express keenness on succumbing to their indigenous belonging to their rulers' mentality and rules of conduct at all costs. They do this by mimicking a similar merging of religion and state and embracing and justifying authoritarian

---

17   van De Beek, A. (2008) 'Christian Identity is Identity in Christ.' In E. Van der Borght (ed.) *Christian Identity*, pp.17–30. Leiden: Brill. De Beek correctly traces the manifestation of the same merging in Modernity Christianity back to Emmanuel Kant's reduction of God into mere necessary postulate for human practical, ultimately and essentially ethical, reasoning activity that is conducted in the service of changing the world (p.20). De Beek might also not be far from the truth when he detects the same phenomenon of merging religion with politics in Christian 'liberation theology, the program for *Justice, Peace and Integrity* of WCC and the anti-conspiracy call of the WARC' (p.23).

power-games and hegemony. Instead of maintaining social credibility and communal acceptance on the basis of a distinction that is expressive of a particular 'Christian' citizenship, these Christians manifest an eagerness to prove to the power-holders their total assimilation and blind loyalty to a divisive and discriminative ruling agenda.

It is far from being foreseeable in the midst of such a challenging identity-compromising setting that Christians could play any credible or trusted mediating role to resolve the clashes in society. It has been hard to find a recent case where Christian Syrian ecclesial leadership reflected in its ministry a genuine perception of the Christian identity as something by means of which the allegiance to Christ-like principles becomes a manifestation of Jesus Christ's action for liberating this leadership and society alike from its occupation with self-centredness. The Christian understanding of Christ's disciples' presence and role in society is remote from the attempt at making one's social presence fall into becoming 'one of the competing ideologies in the world'[18] that measures the Middle Eastern Christians' loyalty and value to their countries by the extent of their assimilation into the political, religious or confessionalist agenda of the ruling powers. This is not really the right way for Christians to enjoy any mediatorial, bridge-building and peacemaking role that can contribute to the recreation of a social harmony in the Middle East. One has to admit here that this context of self-protectionist, confessionalist segregationalism is not the Middle Eastern Christians' own creation in the first place. They found themselves living in the heart of it due to the direly drastic developments in the overall situation of their living-context. Nevertheless, one can still tenably emphasize that gaining an effective presence and role in society does not happen if the Christians enter into the circle of loyalty-proving and favour-gaining of the ruling regimes. Such an option will not merely drive them to lose any neutral mediatorial role in society and avail to them, if ever, only a marginal, insignificant and inconsequential existence in the land. It will, more crucially, drive them to pay the high price of such an existence by means of compromising a particular Christ-like

---

18   van De Beek (2008), p.24.

identity, which lies in the principle of being fully and truly in the world without being of it (John 17.16).

From this perspective, Christians will not be able to contribute to any recreation of social harmony in the Middle East unless they are allowed to do this as a community that is liberated from polarization, confessionalism and self-survival. This liberation is opposite to confessionalism and exclusion. It is a call for breaking free from the ideological divisive boundaries of sectarian self-protectionism and self-enclosure. It is a means for emancipation from hatred, antagonism and partiality by virtue of unity-in-distinction (which is definitive of the Christian understanding of God, the Triune); of 'being fully with' without 'becoming mimically as' the other. Awareness of true identity is not just the starting point of liberation from divisive confessionalism, but also the beginning of playing a unique mediatorial peacemaking role to achieve harmony in societies like the Middle Eastern ones. Succumbing to an obsession with survival, gaining favour and assimilation means compromising Jesus' teaching in John 8.32. Clinging, nevertheless, to a Christ-like identity enables Middle Eastern Christians to launch a publicly praised, trusted and needed mediatorial liberating role in society. It makes them offer it in the service of the people from all backgrounds, communities and societal segments. Christians will be able to play that role if they do not fear power-holders and authorities, and if they call the corrupted, criminal rulers to justice because they are not afraid even if these rulers threaten them with death.[19] It is a fact in today's Syria that the ecclesial Christian prelates do not follow this option. They became part of that confessionalist and divisive atmosphere, instead of abiding with Christ-like principles.

CONCLUSION

As I observe Christians in my homeland, Syria, and in the Middle East in general, I cannot but seriously doubt that Christians have any horizon of presence to enjoy and role to play in their societal existence in the near future in that part of the world. The very present moment in the region relates that the sectarian language

---

19   van De Beek (2008), p.27.

that divides people into fragmented, religious communal cocoons, and almost irremediably reduces people from human citizens in civil society into mere obedient followers in a confessional group, has become the region's habitual, common invective language. In regard to this defect, I see Middle Eastern Christians as totally similar to Middle Eastern Muslims. Remote, like Neptune from Earth, is this language from any language of peace and reconciliation that is required for establishing any social harmony. Remote is this from the language of the Apostle Paul in Galatians 3.28: 'there is no longer Jew or Greek, there is no longer slave or free, there is no longer male and female, for all are one in Christ Jesus'. Paul's teaching is not a message of evangelism that is addressed to others to introduce Christ to them. It is rather a message written to challenge the followers of Christ Jesus themselves and draw their attention to the fact that 'all are one in Christ' means that humans are all equally presented and valued by virtue of their humanity, and not by any narrowly and discriminatively identifying ideology or criterion. Being Christ-like means that Middle Eastern Christians must image that 'all are one' principle in their presence and role within the human existence of the torn-apart contexts of Syria and the Middle East.

It is this biblical language of absolute equality and oneness which Middle Eastern Christians need to abide by if they confess that all humans from all backgrounds, groups and trends suffer equally and face together the same fatefully devastating situation. Advocating such scriptural language and then activating it in reality is what Christians need in my homeland, Syria, to be cured from the venomous poison of confessionalism, societal hatred, religious discrimination and, most importantly, self-minoritization and self-Dhimmitudization.[20] Every time I hear a Christian from Syria or the Middle East use sectarian language, I say to myself: the dividing wall of fear and hostility which

---

20 On self-minoritization and self-Dhimmitudization, see Awad, N.G. (2014b) "an "Ḥimāyat al-Aqaliyyāt" wal-Massīḥiyyīn fī al-Mas'ālah As-Sūriyya' (On 'Minorities-Protection' and the Christians in the Syrian Case). *Almustaqbal Newspaper*, 2 February. Available at www.almustaqbal.com/v4/Article.aspx?Type=np&Articleid=604364, accessed on 21 March 2017; and Awad, N.G. (2014c) 'Theologian: Minority in Syria is Democrats, Liberals from All Religions.' *Syria Direct*, 21 May. Available at www.syriadirect.org/news/theologian-minority-in-syria-is-democrats-liberals-of-all-religions/, accessed on 21 March 2017.

Ephesians 2.14 talks about is being erected again in the region. Confessionalism and sectarian apartheid 'came, divided and victored'. It is the Christians in my homeland before anyone else who should stand committed to, and responsible for, incarnating Paul's words 'all are one in Christ Jesus' in their own presence and role in the midst of the horrible tragedy in the region. It is them, not the non-Christians, who are called by Paul to advocate for this oneness in actual, practical living in the midst of a context of fear, hatred, segregation and violence that seems to be alienating them from the basic content of their own faith.

Chapter Four

A PLACE TO CALL HOME
Middle Eastern Christian Experience of Living
on the Intersection of Two Allegiances

Issa Diab, Lebanon

THE EMERGENCE OF ISLAM IN A
CHRISTIAN MIDDLE EAST

In the atmosphere of Christian disunity and fragmentation,
Islam emerged in the North-West of the Arabian Peninsula
called Najd with its three famous cities: Tā'ef, Mecca and Medina
(previously called Yathreb). Pre-Islamic religions in the Arabian
Peninsula consisted of indigenous polytheistic beliefs, sectarian
Christianity, Judaism and Zoroastrianism. Christian sects were
mostly remains from old Judeo-Christian sects and had Gnostic
and other esoteric beliefs. Some espoused heretical beliefs
such as the Virgin Mary's divinity and the Father–Mother–Son
Trinity. While Ancient Arabian Christianity was strong in areas of
Southern Arabia, with Najrān being an important centre, various
forms of Nestorian Christianity were dominant in Eastern Arabia.
The most prominent Christian sects in the Islamic sources are the
Naṣāra and the Ḥonafā'. These 'heretical' Christian groups had
sought refuge inside the Arabian Peninsula fleeing persecution
led by 'orthodox' Christians as a result of the Christological
conflicts. The prophet of Islam, Muhammad, was himself a fellow
of the Ḥonafā' group. This is the reason why Islam has embraced
much of the doctrines and teachings of Christian sects that were
considered heretical by orthodox Christians.

The formation of Islam did not take a long time (610–632
AD). Islam quickly became a 'socio-religious' entity that will
show its effectiveness in the Arab conquests that will take place

after the death of Muhammad outside the Arab Peninsula. The Islamic Army bounced outside the Arabian Peninsula like the rise of a storm that takes everything in its path. A short time before the death of Muhammad in 632, the Arab conquests outside the Peninsula began, and they intensified during the reign of the first four caliphs (632–662). They oversaw the initial phase of the Muslim conquests, advancing through Persia, Levant, Egypt and North Africa. By 661, Muslim Arabs had taken over the territories assigned to the patriarchates of Alexandria, Antioch and Jerusalem. A century later, the Islamic empire extended from Iberia in the west to the Indus River in the east. Arab Muslims established in the Middle East strong Islamic States such as the Umayyad (662–750), whose capital was Damascus, and the Abbasid (751–1258), whose capital was Baghdad.

Even a long time before the end of the Abbasid state, Islamic States grew up within the central state; some were even stronger than the central state itself. Of these countries, we should mention the Fatimid state (909–1132), during which the Crusaders came to the Middle East (1095–1291); the Ayyubid (1174–1250); the Mamluks (1250–1453); and the Ottomans (1453–1918). These Islamic polities were among the most influential powers in the world.[1]

Existing under the authority of the Islamic State, the Christians of the Middle East began a journey of estrangement from the West. As a result, a wall between East and West started to rise, which reflected negatively on the unity of the Church. The Middle Eastern Christian worldview became largely affected by the Islamic worldview, causing the slide of Arab Christian theologians towards a fundamentalist view of the Bible and its formation.

In the Islamic State, there were different categories of citizens: Arab Muslims, non-Arab Muslims (called *al-mawālī*), People of the Book (Christians, Jews and Zoroastrians) and others. People of the Book were allowed to keep living in the Islamic State but under a particular status. According to Islamic traditions, the

---

1   The author of this article defended a doctoral thesis at the University of Bordeaux, in 2003, entitled, 'Islam is the Inheritor of the Ancient Semitic Civilization'. The thesis was published in more than one book in Arabic. The author believes that Eastern Christianity could not absorb the cultural legacy of the ancient Semitic world. This was done by Islam.

second caliph among the four caliphs, Rāshidoon, 'Umar ben Khattāb (634–644), 'covenanted' the People of the Book to give them freedom of religion while they fulfilled certain conditions. Among others things, they were obliged to pay a *jizya* (tax) for being in the Dhimma (protection) of Muslims. This Dhimmi status of Christians was subject to different interpretations and was a means for degrading them as second-class citizens.

CHRISTIANITY: POSITIVE CONTRIBUTIONS

Despite the major challenges faced by Middle Eastern Christians in their native countries, which had come under Islamic rule, and despite the oppressive laws that they had to live under and all the persecutions they unjustly suffered, the positive impact of Eastern Christians on their societies and peoples was enormous. They expressed their faith by words and attitudes, as well as deeds. When we trace the history of Arab civilization, we can see a significant role for Middle Eastern Christians in two major periods of time: the era of the formation of the Islamic civilization, and the era of the Arabian Renaissance.

Role in the formation of Arab civilization

The Arabs, alongside the conquered peoples, formed the new Islamic civilization. This new civilization was sustained by diverse older cultures that were militarily invaded and yet accepted the new vision of Islamic society. Middle Eastern Christians were among these peoples who founded the Islamic civilization. Antoine Borrut and Fred M. Donner draw the attention of their readers to the very rich contributions of non-Muslims in the administration of the Umayyad state. They highlight how 'the new rulers co-opted the scribes and clerks of the former Sasanian and Byzantine empires to run their tax administration, since they lacked skilled personnel of their own who knew the terrain and the traditional procedures of revenue assessment and collection'.

They add:

> These non-Muslim administrators, and their descendants (since such work tended to run in families), continued to serve in the Umayyad state for over a century, as is visible especially in the rich documentation offered by the Egyptian papyri.[2]

Indeed, during the time of the Umayyad state (662–750), with Damascus as its capital, the Arab rulers asked the Christians to organize and administer the key functions. Borrut and Donner point out that there is scattered evidence that non-Muslims sometimes held positions of real importance. Not a few, it seems, did military service in the Umayyad armies.[3] They add: 'Others were appointed to high-level positions as advisers and administrators; the case of the famous Yuḥannā ibn Sarjūn ibn Manṣūr (d. ca. 131/749), known more generally as Saint John of Damascus, was not unique'.[4] They also show how 'non-Muslims held significant influence in the Umayyad regime, perhaps even in the formulation of policy'.[5]

According to the Arabic Annals of the 'Melkite' Christian historian Eutychios of Alexandria (877–940), Manṣūr (the grandfather) had been appointed a tax official in Damascus by the Byzantine emperor Maurice (582–602). During the Persian occupation (614–628), again according to Eutychios, Manṣūr had remitted the taxes collected during the occupation to the Persian authorities. This was the reason for disagreement with the Byzantines. Eutychios told that when the Arab Muslim leader Khāled ibn al-Walid came to Damascus, Manṣūr's dispute with the Byzantines was at its peak. He agreed to deliver the city to the Arabs against privileges from them for the freedom of worship

---

2   Borrut, A. and Donner, F.M. (2016) 'Introduction: Christians and Others in the Umayyad State.' In A. Borrut and F.M. Donner (eds) *Christians and Others in the Umayyad State*, LAMINE 1 (Late Antique and Medieval Islamic Near East, number 1), p.1. Chicago, IL: The Oriental Institute of the University of Chicago.

3   The authors refer to Wadād al-Qāḍī's paper in the same volume.

4   The authors refer to Muriel Debié's contribution to the same volume, especially on Athanasius bar Gūmōyē.

5   Griffith, S.H. (2016) 'The Manṣūr Family and Saint John of Damascus: Christians and Muslims in Umayyad Times.' In A. Borrut and F.M. Donner (eds) *Christians and Others in the Umayyad State*, LAMINE 1 (Late Antique and Medieval Islamic Near East, number 1), p.30. Chicago, IL: The Oriental Institute of the University of Chicago.

for Christians.[6] Eutychios wrote on this in detail transmitting to us the agreement between Manṣūr and the Muslim leader, Khalid.[7]

So begins the story of the Christian Manṣūr family's association with the Muslims in Damascus at the very beginning of Muslim rule. Members of the family reappear in Christian accounts of life in Damascus and in Jerusalem under the rule of the Umayyads (662–750), extending even into the beginnings of the Abbasid times (750 and beyond). The Manṣūrs were an indigenous Christian family whose members enjoyed a high civil status, both under Byzantine rule and under the Umayyads. 'In all likelihood, given the evidence of their name, the Manṣūr family was of Aramaean, maybe even Arab, stock.'[8] According to the Arab historian al-Yaʿqūbī, none of the caliphs before Muʿāwiya I (661–680) had employed Christians in their service.[9] Muʿāwiya was said to have inaugurated the practice, which would become a commonplace administrative arrangement among later caliphs and Muslim governors, reaching well into Abbasid times and beyond.[10]

Manṣūr's son, known in the sources as Sarjūn ibn Manṣūr, came into particular favour during the lifetime of Muʿāwiya's son, Yazīd I (c. 680–683). Reports even spoke of Sarjūn and the Christian court poet Akhṭal as Yazīd's table companions from his

6   Eutychios, *Annales*; see editions by Breydy; Cheïkho, Carra de Vaux, and Zayyat; and Pirone. A Latin translation by John Selden under the title *Contextio gemmarum* appears in Migne, ed., *Patrologia graeca*, vol. 111. Quoted in Borrut and Donner (2016), p.29.
7   Breydy (ed.), Eutychios, Annales, (Arabic), Corpus Scriptorum Christianorum Orientalium (CSCO) 471, pp.137–138, CSCO 472, pp.116–117 in the German translation. See the comments on this account in Lammens, 'Études sur le règne du Calife Omaiyade Moʿawia Ier (troisième série),' pp.250–257. Quoted in Borrut and Donner (2016), p.30.
8   Borrut and Donner (2016), pp.2–3.
9   See al-Yaʿqūbī, *Taʾrīkh*, vol. 2, p.265. Quoted in Griffith (2016), p.31.
10   See Louis Cheïkho (1987) *Les vizirs et secrétaires arabes chrétiens en Islam (622–1517), Patrimoine Arabe Chrétien 11*. Jounieh: Librairie Saint-Paul; Rome: Pontificio Istituto Orientale. See also Louis Massignon (1942) 'La politique islamo-chrétienne des scribes nestoriens de Deir Qunna à la cour de Bagdad au ixe siècle de notre ère.' *Vivre et Penser 2*, 7–14; Jason R. Zaborowski (2011) 'Arab Christian Physicians as Interreligious Mediators: Abū Shākir as a Model Christian Expert.' *Islam and Muslim-Christian Relations 22*, 85–96. All these references are quoted in Griffith (2016), p.31.

youth.[11] And the sources mention a number of events in caliphal history in this period in which Sarjūn was said to have been involved, reaching well into the reign of the caliph, ʿAbd al-Malik (685–705).[12] Sarjūn's son, known in the sources as Manṣūr ibn Sarjūn, was the member of the family who would, in due course, come to be known as Saint John of Damascus; it seemed likely that he took the name John on becoming a monk in Jerusalem.

John of Damascus was among the earliest of the Christian writers in the conquered territories to take the religious challenge of the Arab conquest seriously. His response to the challenge unfolded the Umayyad programme to claim the political body for Islam and the rapidly growing confrontation between Christians and Muslims more broadly, in the time Islam was thought to be a Christian sect. John of Damascus framed a comprehensive approach to the developing religious thinking among Muslim intellectuals in his days. Their thinking would have impacted the Christian communities; their writings would have imparted to Muslims, in their interactions with contemporary Jews and Christians, their increasing tendency to call others to the profession of Islam (the Islamic *daʿwa*).

Another contemporary family distinguished itself during the same period. The Gūmōyē family of Edessa[13] was the counterpart of the Manṣūr family of Damascus, as well as their religious adversaries, since they were Syriac Orthodox, non-Chalcedonians, while the Manṣūrs were Chalcedonian Melkites. The Manṣūrs were at the caliph's court in Damascus and the Gūmōyē in Egypt. The two Christian families, although belonging to antagonistic

---

11   See in particular the studies of Henri Lammens: 'Études sur le règne du Calife Omaiyade Moʿawia 1re (troisième série)', 'Le califat de Yazid 1re', 'Le chantre des Omiades'. See also Suzanne Pinckney Stetkevych's chapter 'Al-Akhṭal at the Court of ʿAbd al-Malik: The Qaṣīda and the Construction of Umayyad Authority' in Antoine Borrut and Fred M. Donner (2016).

12   See Cheïkho, *Les vizirs et secrétaires*, pp.73–74. The Byzantine chronicler Theophanes the Confessor (ca. 760–815) reports that when ʿAbd al-Malik wanted to take some pillars away from the church at Gethsemane in Palestine to incorporate them into a building in Mecca, 'Now Sergius, son of Mansour, a good Christian, who was treasurer and stood on close terms with Abimelech [i.e. ʿAbd al-Malik]', persuaded him against this course of action (Theophanes, *Chronicle*, p.510). Quoted in Griffith (2016), p.31.

13   See Debié, M. (2016) 'Christians in the Service of the Caliph: Through the Looking Glass of Communal Identities.' In A. Borrut and F.M. Donner (eds) *Christians and Others in the Umayyad State*, LAMINE 1 (Late Antique and Medieval Islamic Near East, number 1), pp.54–56. Chicago, IL: The Oriental Institute of the University of Chicago.

Christian churches, should have been in touch since they were part of the same Umayyad administration, and probably had at some point to work together. Dionysius' fairly long account of the life and career of Athanasius bar Gūmōyē in the caliph's service was preserved in the later chronicle of Michael the Syrian.[14]

Debié tells us that there can be little doubt that it was precisely because of their skills, developed by a careful education that, at the time of the nascent Umayyad empire when competent civil servants were urgently required, the Christian nobles were employed as secretaries and administrators despite their religion.[15]

Also during the Umayyad state, Christians offered services in education to the Muslim Arabs. Sources indicate that the Syriac non-Chalcedonian Christians used to build religious buildings used as churches or monasteries and, beside them, schools. One example could be found in the Syriac *Life of Simeon of the Olives*, a monk of the celebrated monastery of Mar-Gabriel/Qartmin, who later became the bishop of Ḥarrān.[16] While still a monk, but one with a private fortune, Simeon decided to build churches for the Syriac Orthodox community in the city of Nisibis (modern Nusaybin in south-east Turkey), which had traditionally been a stronghold of the Nestorians. He gained support from the local Muslim governor through his generous gifts and got permission from the caliph. The opposition he encountered did not come, as might have been expected, from the Muslim authorities but from the Nestorians, who were at that time the dominant Christian group in the city and who were hostile to the local implantation of the Syriac Orthodox with the support of the Muslim authorities. Simeon allegedly also built a mosque in the city with a *madrasa* (school), just as he had founded a school with the church in his native village of Habsenas.

The 'classical' culture of the golden age of the Abbasids (775–861) was the apogee of the Islamic civilization. A thirst for knowledge, any knowledge, was a hallmark of the Abbasid rule.

---

14   Michael the Syrian, *Chronicle*, ed. Chabot, XI, 16, t. IV, pp.447–448 T, II, p.475; Michael the Syrian, *Chronicle up to the Year 1234*, ed. Chabot, I, pp.229–230 T, 294–295 V. See Debié (2016), p.55.
15   See Debié (2016), p.56.
16   See Debié (2016), pp.58–59.

Contacts with China, India, Persia and Eurasia were important in developing sciences and culture in the growing Islamic empire. Translations of Greek, Sanskrit and Syriac works were common and familiarized Islamic civilization with the ideas of Galen, Ptolemy, Euclid, Aristotle, Plato and the Neo-Platonists' Syriac fathers. Middle Eastern Christians made great contributions to the translations from Greek and Syriac into Arabic. By doing this, they would have introduced the Muslims to Greek learning and to the eminent Greek scientists and philosophers. They also introduced them to the Aramaic culture in its two forms: Syriac and Assyrian. Eastern Christians (particularly Nestorian Christians) contributed to the Arab Islamic Civilization during the Umayyad and the Abbasid periods by translating works of Greek philosophers into Syriac and afterwards into Arabic.[17] They also excelled in philosophy, science, theology and medicine.[18] Muslims had little knowledge of languages other than Arabic. Consequently, the translators of Greek and other non-Muslim scientific works into Arabic were never Muslims. They were Christians of the three dominant Eastern denominations, plus a few Jews and Sabians. The languages of liturgy and culture for these Christians were Syriac or Assyrian (Syro-Aramaic or eastern Aramaic) and their liturgical language was Greek, but they also had the skill of communication in Arabic. Rémi Brague writes:

> Neither were there any Muslims among the ninth-century translators. Almost all of them were Christians of various eastern denominations: Jacobites, Melchites, and, above all, Nestorians... A few others were Sabians... No Muslim learned Greek or, even less, Syriac. Cultivated Christians were often bilingual, even trilingual: they used Arabic for daily life, Syriac for liturgy, and Greek for cultural purposes. The translators that helped to pass along the Greek heritage to the Arabs were artisans who worked for private patrons, without institutional support.[19]

---

17 Hill, D. (1993) *Islamic Science and Engineering*, p.4. Edinburgh: Edinburgh University Press.

18 Rémi Brague 'Assyrians Contributions to the Islamic Civilization.' Available at www.christiansofiraq.com/assyriancontributionstotheislamiccivilization.htm, accessed 9 September 2016.

19 Rémi Brague, *The Legend of the Middle Ages*, 2009, p.164. Retrieved 9 September, 2016.

Brague sees the stories, that are told about the 'house of wisdom' (*bayt al-hikmah*), a kind of research centre subsidized by the caliphs that specialized in producing Arabic translations of Greek works, as pure legend.[20] Karl Kaser writes about the centres of learning and of transmission of classical wisdom that were founded by Christians in monasteries or in eminent Christian cities. These centres included colleges, such as the School of Nisibis, the School of Edessa (Urfa – also called the Academy of Athens, a Christian theological and medical university) and the renowned hospital and medical academy of Jundishapur.[21] He also speaks about libraries – including the Library of Alexandria and the Imperial Library of Constantinople – and other centres of translation and learning that functioned at Merv, Salonika, Nishapur and Ctesiphon, situated just south of what later became Baghdad.[22] Christian Nestorians played a prominent role in the translation work of this institution which made great contributions to the formation of Arab culture. Notably, eight generations of the Nestorian Bukhtishu family served as private doctors to caliphs and sultans between the eighth and eleventh centuries.[23]

Christian Nestorians excelled in philosophy and science (Hunayn ibn Ishaq, Qusta ibn Luqa, Masawaiyh, Patriarch Eutychius, Jabril ibn Bukhtishu, etc.) and theology (Tatian, Bar Daisan, Babai the Great, Nestorius, Toma bar Yacoub, etc.); the personal physicians of the Abbasid caliphs were often Assyrian Christians, such as the long-serving Bukhtishu dynasty.[24] Thus, when Islam emerged and Muslims conquered the surrounding countries, the cultural and scientific context was already founded mainly by Christians. Thus, Christian contribution was needed to

---

20   Rémi Brague, *The Legend of the Middle Ages*, 2009, p.164. Retrieved 9 September, 2016.
21   The city of Gundeshapur was founded in 271 by the Sassanid king Shapur I. It was one of the major cities in Khuzestan province of the Persian empire in what is today Iran.
22   Kaser, K. (2011) *The Balkans and the Near East: Introduction to a Shared History*, p.135. Berlin: Lit Verlag.
23   Bonner, B., Ener, M. and Singer, A. (2003) *Poverty and Charity in Middle Eastern Contexts*, p.97. Albany, NY: SUNY Press. Ruano, E.B. and Burgos, M.E. (1992) *17e Congrès international des sciences historiques: Madrid, du 26 août au 2 septembre 1990*, p.527. Madrid: Comité international des sciences historiques.
24   Rémi Brague, "Assyrians contributions to the Islamic civilisation", op.cit.

translate this legacy into Arabic and to form what later became the 'Islamic civilization'.

A striking example of the importance of communal affiliations in the transmission of historical information within the Christian communities as much as between Christians and Muslims was provided by the person and work of Theophilus of Edessa (ca. 695–785).[25] He has attracted much attention in recent decades and exemplifies how the transmission of knowledge was much more dependent on the Christian affiliations than on translation from one language to another or from one religion to another. Theophilus had been known for a long time to specialists of astrology as one of the leading Christian astrologers, whose works written in Greek entered the great Byzantine collections and also had a strong influence on Islamic astrology.[26] He was the – or one of the – official astronomers of the caliph al-Mahdī (775–785) in Baghdad and might previously have been in the service of Marwān II (744–750) in the same capacity.[27]

One prominent translator was the Christian scholar Hunayn ibn ishaq (808–873), called Johannitius in Latin. He was a Nestorian (Assyrian) Christian who had studied Greek in Greek lands and eventually settled in Baghdad. He, together with his son and his nephew, translated into Arabic, sometimes from Syriac, Galen's medical treatises as well as Hippocratic works and texts by Aristotle, Plato and others. His own compositions included the ten treatises on the eye, which transmitted a largely Galenic theory of vision. This is not to underestimate the work of Thabit ibn qurra (ca. 836–901), a Sabian, in translating many Greek books of philosophy and science, and the works of Al-kindi (d. ca. 873) and Al-Farabi (ca. 875–950), both of whom were Muslims.

---

25 See Debié (2016), pp.65ff.
26 On the successive developments of this story, see Brock, S.P (1982) 'Transformations of the Edessa Portrait.' In G.H.A. Juynboll (ed.) *Studies in the First Century of Islamic Society*, Papers on Islamic History 5. Carbondale, IL: Southern Illinois University Press, 1982. Reported by Debié (2016), p.65.
27 David Pingree, 'From Alexandria to Baghdād to Byzantium: The Transmission of Astrology', *International Journal of the Classical Tradition* 8/1 (2001): 3–37, p.15. Reported by Debié (2016), p.66.

Role in the Renaissance of the Arab civilization

It is true that Islamic civilization reached its apogee at about the end of the first millennium, and its shadow continued in the following century. However, the rise of the Tantalite Islamic literalism in the tenth century, the defeat of the Mu'tazalite free thinking school, and the renewal of the Hanbalite Fundamentalist school in the thought of ibn Taymiyyah's fundamentalist thinking and his disciple ibn Qayyim al-Jawziya's fundamentalist jurisprudence in the twelfth century made Islamic civilization shrink back rapidly.

After the withdrawal of the Crusaders from the Middle East about the end of the thirteenth century, the Muslim Mamluks turned against Christians and began persecuting them fiercely because they accused them of helping the Crusaders. A number of Christians had to flee to Cyprus and the neighbouring countries where the Mamluks could not reach them and a number of them fled to the mountains and rugged places, and hid themselves in caves where they lived until the end of the Mamluk regime. The Ottomans behaved no better.

Education among Christians was very weak. There was an almost illiterate clergy. Because of the persecutions of the Mamluks and then the Ottomans, Christian religious leaders isolated themselves for security reasons. Every Christian community used its ethnic language (Syriac, Coptic and Armenian) for communication and liturgical matters. The use of Arabic in their prayers was very weak. Muslims frequently criticized the liturgies of the Christians for containing bad Arabic. This adaptation of 'Christian Arabic' that is widely different from Islamic Arabic constituted a psychological barrier between Christians and Muslims. By the sixteenth century, both Muslims and Christians in the Middle East experienced the 'Dark Age' at all levels: economic, cultural and educational. This was at a time when Europe entered the Renaissance and the Reformation eras. In the seventeenth century Catholic missionary agencies started coming to work in the Middle East. They were followed by Protestants in the eighteenth century. These Western Christians founded schools, universities and other humanitarian organizations. These Christian educational institutions provided the Middle Eastern Christians with Western culture and helped them rise from their 'Dark Age'. Christians could also help their Muslim co-citizens get out of the 'Dark Age' too.

Prior to the coming of these missionary societies, there were only primitive schools, run by local Christian churches, which provided a poor education to a very limited number of students. In addition, Islamic and Ottoman culture prevented women from accessing education, and the Middle Eastern Christian community at that time was affected by this culture. The Ottoman authority, that was promoting the Turkic culture, prohibited Arab Christians to write religious books in Arabic; hence, Christians wrote their books with Syriac alphabets.

The participation of the enlightened Middle Eastern Christians in the development of their societies was enormous and took several forms. Christian schools and universities founded in the Middle East got international good reputations and academic recognition. Students (mainly Christians) who studied in these institutions learned sciences and new technologies, and were trained in free and critical thinking. They acquired their feeling of nationalism in these Christian universities. Those Christians, mainly from Lebanon, Syria and Egypt, instigated what we call now the 'Arab Renaissance'. This was a 'Renaissance' of Arab culture. It began in the late nineteenth and early twentieth centuries. Beirut, Cairo, Damascus and Aleppo were the main centres of this Renaissance. It led to the establishment of national schools, universities, printing presses and publishing houses. It was during this stage that the first compound of the Arabic language was introduced along with the printing of it in Arabic letters. The Arab Renaissance covered all areas related to life, society and being: art, science, humanities, culture, education, economics, journalism, emancipation of women, human rights and other social issues.

In the field of Arabic language, the Arab Renaissance led to the renewal of literary, linguistic and poetic forms of the Arabic language and literature, in ways that presented its distinctiveness. Arabic grammar was standardized in a modern form. In politics and social sciences, the establishment of civic societies gave birth to the idea of Arab nationalism and the demand for reformation of the Ottoman Empire, which led to a calling for the establishment of modern states based on the European style. In sum, the Arab Renaissance during the late Ottoman rule was, as Michael

Teague puts it, a quantum leap to post-industrial revolution.[28] It cannot be limited to the fields of cultural, economic and political renaissance. It was a whole and radical change of society and of identity. It was extended to include the whole spectrum of society.

It is true that the impact of the Renaissance on the Christian community was stronger than on Muslims because this Renaissance emerged from Christian institutions, but it did also have an impact on Muslims. For this reason, Muslim reformists (including Jamal ed-Dine el-Afghani, Mohammad Abdo and Ali Abdulrazeq), being impacted by a new epistemology, raised and started reformation work in Islam itself.

Arab Renaissance can be divided into three stages, and each stage had its enlightened pioneers. The first stage took place in the sixteenth and seventeenth centuries, and the second surfaced in contemporary culture during the eighteenth and nineteenth centuries; the final stage played its role around the end of the nineteenth and early twentieth centuries. The Christians of the first stage (sixteenth and seventeenth centuries) had their education in the West (Rome and Paris) where they studied Christian theology and the ramifications of philosophical knowledge that was dominated by the European religious and philosophical thought. During that period, the famous Maronite School in Rome emerged (1584), and later, Napoleon Bonaparte transferred it to Paris by force during one of his conquests in Italy (1798). The importance of this school lay in the political role which built a historic and cultural bridge of cooperation between Europe and the Levant, at a time when Europe was witnessing contemporary religious and ideological transformations. Furthermore, the Maronite School in Rome and Paris played a significant role in the purification of the Orientalist thought of those mistakes, myths and encroachment on Islam and Arab history. The students of the School (Arab Christians) clarified a lot of uncertainty and corrected wrong ideas about Arabs and Islam, which were dominated by European thinkers through debates or research and translations. This contributed to clarifying areas which were previously unexplained or unclear, either because of language (errors in translation) or duplicate meanings, or as a

---

28   Teague, M. (2010) 'The new Christian question.' *Al Jadid Magazine 16*, 62.

result of ignorance and intolerance. In this way, Arab Christians would have provided great services to Islam and Muslims.

Among the most prominent philosophers of the seventeenth century was Father Peter al-Toulāwi, a Christian cleric from Batrūn (Lebanon), a graduate of the Maronite School in Rome in 1669. At that time, the curriculum of the School contained languages (Arabic, Italian, French and ancient languages like Greek and Syriac), theology, philosophy and logic. The methodology of teaching was European, founded by St Thomas Aquinas, and was affected positively and negatively by the Islamic philosophy of Al-Fārābi, ibn Sīna, Al-Ghazali and ibn Rushd. Because of this hidden link between Greek philosophy, the philosophy of the Arab-Islamic and European philosophy in its first stage, a strong base for systematic historical correlation between the three civilizations was formed. After his return to Lebanon in 1682, Patriarch Stephan Doueihy gave Father Toulāwi the responsibility of teaching in the Maronite School in Aleppo that was founded in 1666 as an extension to the School in Rome. He died in 1746 after educating a large number of students over more than half a century. The second generation of the founders of the Arab Renaissance built on the foundations laid by the first generation. These were the students of the first generation who graduated from the village school. Among them was the poet Nassif al-Yāzji (Greek Catholic), who was born in the village of Kafrshīma (Mount Lebanon) in 1800. He had his first education from his father, and finished his studies in the school of the Lebanese Maronite Order.

Another example is the thinker Ahmad Faris Shidyaq (Maronite converted to Islam) who was born in 1805 in the village of Achkout then moved to Hadath (near Beirut) and entered the Maronite School of Aïn Waraqa. This latter school formed generations of Christian thinkers. Many continued their studies in other Christian schools and universities. Among them was al-Mu'allim (teacher) Boutros al-Boustany who was born in the village of al-Doubbiyyeh in the Chouf district (Lebanon) in 1819. He studied in the famous Aïn Waraqa School and in other schools that were opened by Christian missions. He converted to Protestantism and worked with the first missionaries where he learned the Western Anglophone educational philosophy. He participated with Eli

Smith and Cornelius Van Dayck in the translation of the Bible into Arabic. This translation, which is still used by the majority of Eastern Christians and Evangelical Churches, contributed to the Arab Renaissance in many ways and caused a spiritual revival in Middle Eastern Christianity. The two Christian thinkers, Chidiac and al-Bustani, were a very important phenomenon in the context of the history of the first nucleus of contemporary Arab thought that played a political role at the end of the nineteenth and early twentieth centuries. The importance of Chidiac and al-Bustani was that they tried to transfer their ideas from thought to action, raising awareness through field activity and the establishment of schools and the publication of newspapers. This transition from thought to action was an important step in the formation of institutions which were independent from Western missions; these independent institutions aspired to produce graduates whose nationalistic thinking would contribute to efforts to save the national identity from religion and religious identity. This marked the beginning of awareness of what was known later as secularism and attempts to separate religion from the state and national identity from national religion. The two Christians, Chidiac and al-Bustani, the two graduates of Aïn Waraqa School, a Lebanese Maronite school, were instrumental in developing the type of thinking that would lead to the Arab Renaissance.

At this time, the first Christian colleges and universities in the Middle East were founded. During the eighteenth century, the Church of England mission and the German Lutheran Church opened schools in Palestine. In 1863, Robert College was founded in Bebek (Turkey) by Christopher Robert, a wealthy American and a philanthropist, and Cyrus Hamlin, a missionary devoted to education. The American Protestant missionaries established, in 1866, the Syrian Evangelical College in Beirut, which became later known as the American University of Beirut. In 1875, the Jesuit Order opened Saint Joseph University. These two Christian universities employed the best qualified people and the highest thinkers from the whole Arab World. Thus, Aïn Waraqa School, in addition to Aïntoura School and the network of educational institutions administered by the Maronite Order and other Christian schools, colleges and universities founded by Christian missions in the Arab Mashreq formed the nucleus of the cultured elite in the Arab World, who played a role, starting from the third generation, in the formation of contemporary thought that developed nationalist and secular ideologies such as national socialism, emancipation of women and other streams and theories transmitted or adapted from European schools and still valid even today. This generation also established syndicates and started a very rudimentary form of democracy. These Christian educational institutions played a leading role in the development of the Arab civilization and culture.[29]

The third and last generation of the Arab Renaissance founders was formed of Christian thinkers who played a historical role in the revival of Arab heritage and literature. There are many famous names in Arabic thought and literature. Examples are: Gibran Khalil Gibran, the author of *The Prophet* and the third bestselling poet of all time, behind Shakespeare and Laozi; Mikhail Naima, a philosopher and poet who wrote *Eyelid Whisperings*; May Ziadeh, a pioneer of oriental feminism; and Ameen Rihani, Lebanese intellectual and political activist. In the press emerged Georgy Zeidan, founder of the *al-Hilāl* (Crescent) magazine in 1892; Yacoub Sarraf, founder of the newspaper *Moqattam* in Egypt; Salīm al-'Anjawi, founder of the *mir'āt al-Sharq* (Mirror of the East) magazine; Iskandar Shalhoub, founder of the Sultanate's magazine in 1879; and Saleem Takla and his brother Bishara Takla, founders of the Cairo newspaper *Al-Ahram*.[30] Among the Christian pioneers in theatre were Maroun Abboud and Maroun Naccache, who contributed to the growing theatre movement in Egypt. Also, the Christian Francis Marrash introduced the use of the mind in everything and mainly in religion. He further proclaimed freedom and equality, and the struggle against tyranny and slavery. He demanded that the nation should belong to everyone. Adīb Ishaq opposed foreign colonialism and intervention and called for Arab unity. Farah Anton translated many books into Arabic and authored several books of public importance. Arab Christians led Muslims in opposing the movement of Turkification that was very active around the time of the end of the Ottoman Empire.

---

29 Lattouf, M. (2004) *Women, Education, and Socialization In Modern Lebanon: 19th and 20th Centuries Social History*, p.70. Lanham, MD: University Press of America.

30 A. Fisher Merrill, Harold John Calhoun, *The world's great dailies: profiles of fifty newspapers*, LA University of Michigan, p.52, Reported by https://en.wikipedia.org/wiki/Arab_Christians, accessed 28 September 2016.

In the post-Ottoman era, some of the most influential Arab nationalists were Arab Christians, like the Syrian historian Constantin Zureiq and the two Syrian politicians, Michel 'Aflaq and Fares al-Khoury. Several Arab Christians edited the leading newspapers in Mandatory Palestine including *Falastin*, edited by the Isa brothers, and *al-Karmīl*, which was edited by Najīb Nassar. Khalil al-Sakakini, a prominent Jerusalemite, was also an Arab Orthodox, as was George Antonius, author of *The Arab Awakening*.

Present and future prospects

Now, after centuries of interaction with Muslims, Middle Eastern Christians, a majority that was rendered to a minority, even a suffering minority, live an uncertain present going towards an uncertain future. Numbers of Christians are decreasing dramatically across the Middle East, in Syria, Iraq, Palestine, Jordan and Egypt.

I concur with Jane Smith's analysis of the present situation of Middle Eastern Christians with their Muslim co-citizens. Smith speaks about the unforgettable history in these words:

> Muslim expansion into Christian territories and Christian imperialism in Muslims' lands have fostered fear and ill-will on both sides. Repercussions from the Crusades continue to resound in the contemporary rhetoric employed by defenders of both faiths.[31]

She also describes realistically the theological image each community has of the other:

> While a number of verses in the Qur'an call for treating Christians and Jews with respect as recipients of God's divine message, in reality many Muslims have found it difficult not to see Christians as polytheists because of their doctrine of the Trinity. Christians, for their part, traditionally have viewed the Qur'an as fraudulent and Muhammad as an imposter.[32]

---

31 Smith, J. (2015) 'Muslim-Christian Relations: Historical and Contemporary Realities.' Available at http://religion.oxfordre.com/view/10.1093/acrefore/9780199340378. 001.0001/acrefore-9780199340378-e-11, accessed on 17 August 2016.
32 Smith (2015).

The USA and other Western democracies have signed protection treaties with Arab polities in the Arab Gulf, which are like 'family corporations', in order to benefit from the oil concessions in return, overlooking the rights of religious minorities. They allied with Islamic fundamentalist societies, such as the Muslim Brotherhood, to use them as a tool for political change, even in the most secular regimes in the Arab World. This resulted in abductions, torture and violence against Christians, including the bombing of churches, the displacement of Christians, and the threat of extinction for historic Churches in their regions of historical existence. The first invasion of Iraq in 2003 was followed by the second invasion, the war in Afghanistan, and the so-called Arab Spring which turned into a violent autumn and winter. All these factors generated displacement and genocide of Christians and a dramatic weakening of the Middle Eastern historical Churches. It is possible that the long-term consequences of these events and the ensuing chaos that followed will make Middle Eastern Christianity history and its institutions museums. The political behaviour of the 'Christian' West towards the Muslim Middle East, that prioritizes economic interests and does not take into account social justice and people's rights, has negative aftershocks for the Christians of the Middle East.

This is exactly what is happening to Middle Eastern Christians: displacement of their historic Churches and institutions from places they have occupied for thousands of years to an unknown port and unknown destiny; large numbers of Christians fled from Iraq, Syria, Egypt, Jordan and Palestine as a result of the so-called Arab Spring. By doing this, the 'Christian' West contributes to the ongoing displacement of Middle Eastern Christians from their territories, which has been their painful experience since the seventh century. All the Eastern Christian Churches and the major Western Churches are represented in Jerusalem, whose holy places have been the goal of Christian pilgrimage since the fourth century. But Jerusalem is heading towards being empty of Christians. There may come a time when Christians will be owners of buildings and shrines in the Middle East but have no people or presence. Enlightened Muslims see that a Middle East without its Middle Eastern Christians will be an awful Middle East. El-Hassan bin Talal, Crown Prince of Jordan, wrote in 1995:

Much concern about the future of the Christian Arabs is currently being expressed in international circles and the international media. Also, much fear of the future is being voiced among Christians inside the Arab World, particularly in connection with the waves of Islamic fundamentalism which have been sweeping a number of Arab countries during the last decade. People who entertain such concern or fear rarely take into account that it is in the nature of waves, no matter their apparent enormity, to subside once they have consumed their initial driving force, especially in the case of waves of social behaviour driven by ephemeral emotion rather than by solid reason. The fact remains that the Christian Arabs are in no way aliens to Muslim Arab society: a society whose history and culture they have shared for over fourteen centuries to date, without interruption, and to whose material and moral civilization they have continually contributed, and eminently so, on their own initiative or by trustful request.[33]

Since 1994, the 'Fundamentalism Waves' have not subsided as Prince Hassan expected. These waves are growing and becoming more dangerous and threatening the future of the Middle Eastern Christians. I have no doubt that these Islamic fundamentalist waves are serious and authentic, but they are also a political game. I mean political intelligences are exploiting religion to create a chaotic status in the Middle East. And Middle Eastern Christians are paying the price of this game.

CONCLUSION

How should Middle Eastern Christians' behave actively and postively facing persecutions and challenges to avoid being lonely and isolated? Christians' emigration from the Middle East, as is currently taking place, is not the best solution. We should learn from Church history that the strength of Christianity is not in the numbers of Christians but in the amount of Christian authenticity lived by Christians. Christianity is a religion of service and love; love is giving and forgiving. Christianity is a religion of sacrifice

---

33   Bin Talal, H. (1994) *Christianity in the Arab World*, pp.97–98. Amman: Royal Institute for Inter-Faith Studies.

and martyrdom. Christianity is the religion of the Cross. Prince
Hassan says it in his way:

> With such a heritage of trust and good faith in their favour,
> Christian Arabs need not feel any more apprehensive than
> other Arabs of things to come. With the patience, resilience
> and empathy for which they have been historically known, and
> the imaginative leadership they have rarely lacked, they will
> surely be at no loss to find their place in the Arab world of the
> future, to their own benefit, and to the benefit of all other parties
> concerned.[34]

One of the resolutions of the Special Assembly of the Synod of
Bishops for the Middle East, that took place in Rome from 10–24
October 2010, was that studying the Bible helps Christians to cling
to the Christian testimony in their own land. The synod asked the
churches to organize a yearly 'week of the Bible' to encourage
believers to read the Bible and to help them apply its teaching in
their daily lives.

The Fathers of the Synod believe that interest in the Bible
stimulates spiritual life, strengthens the Christian testimony in an
environment that needs to recognize Christianity with its roots,
and affirms Christians in their land despite all the injustices,
hardships and challenges. The Bible renews the vision and opens
the eyes to new needs in the new situation of the region.

---

34   Bin Talal (1994), p.98.

Chapter Five

MIGRATION, DUAL IDENTITY AND INTEGRATION
A Christian Approach to Embracing Others
across Enduring Lines of Difference

C.A. Strine, Sheffield, UK

INTRODUCTION

One of the very first things Donald Trump did at the outset of
his presidency was to announce restrictions on travel to the
United States from seven countries in the Middle East. His order
drew particular attention to the policy for identifying, vetting,
and resettling refugees in the United States. At the same time,
the discourse in the United Kingdom around stresses upon the
National Health Service and state schools frequently references
the number of migrants in the country as an important factor
putting such services under massive pressure, albeit with
other contributing factors. Within days of Donald Trump's
announcement, the UK government announced it would stop
resettling unaccompanied minors requesting refugee status.
Wherever one looks in the news media, one finds issues related,
more or less obviously, to questions around the arrival and
integration of new migrants into societies.

Indeed, in the United Kingdom two high profile reports
on integration were released near the end of 2016. First was
the government commissioned Casey Review, examining the
opportunities for migrants living in the UK and their integration
into British society. Among its wide-ranging findings, the Casey
Review concluded that high rates of transnational marriage may
undermine the process of immigrants integrating into their host
communities. Further, the Casey Review highlighted a Demos

study showing that over 50 per cent of ethnic minority students were in schools where ethnic minorities conversely formed the majority of students. Casey worried that this situation insulates these students from a critical opportunity to build positive links with the wider community.[1] Such situations no doubt influence public perception. Casey noted polling data from 2015 which showed that 55 per cent of the British public agreed there was a clash between Islam and the values of British society. Likewise, 46 per cent of Muslims felt their lives in the UK were made more difficult by prejudice against Islam.[2]

The second report came from the All Party Parliamentary Group on Integration. That document contends that in many parts of the UK 'immigrant communities and members of the settled population are leading parallel rather than interconnected lives'.[3] Noting unprecedented levels of immigration to the UK since 2004, the report concludes that the UK has 'witnessed growing inequalities, rapid technological advancements and cuts to public and voluntary sector services which have tended to undermine opportunities for social mixing and for the integration of newcomers'.[4]

These reports underscore that there is an active public debate about the integration of migrants into receiving cultures in the United Kingdom. This public discourse reflects the broader international situation where so-called developed nations are actively formulating responses to what people and their political representatives see as a crucial issue with a wide range of negative consequences as a result of it. While much is being said, one cannot escape the sense that all this discussion has produced no more than a series of ad hoc responses. Producing coherent views and policy positions requires a more measured approach that identifies deep convictions about how to address the issues raised by high rates of migration. Here, these pressing

1   Casey, L. (2016) 'The Casey Review: A Review into Opportunity and Integration (Executive Summary)', p.11. London: Department for Communities and Local Government.
2   Casey (2016), pp.12–13. Of course, what constitutes 'British society' is not specified, which is lamentable. This corresponds with statements often found in the media about British values, an undefined and surely heterogeneous concept.
3   Kere, A. and Bell, R. (2017) 'All Party Parliamentary Group on Social Integration: Interim Report into Integration of Immigrants', p.3. Available at www.socialintegrationappg.org.uk/reports, accessed on 11 February 2017.
4   Kere and Bell (2017), p.25.

questions can be framed even more specifically, namely, asking what would constitute a distinctively Christian response to the current worldwide proliferation of migration.[5]

Christians of all denominations recognize the importance of the Bible in framing their understanding of and response to such issues, even if the specific role Scripture plays will be framed differently across Christian traditions. In this essay, a range of biblical material relating to migration will be discussed, providing a basis upon which to outline a Christian approach to responding to the issues surrounding the integration of migrants into host societies. The diverse statements in the Old and New Testaments, it shall be argued, indicate that both hosts and migrants have obligations to the other group that should promote embracing those from different backgrounds without eliminating enduring differences between them. Furthermore, the Bible outlines a view of Christian identity that supersedes national identity without eliminating its role; this relationship has consequences for Christians among host groups. Finally, the duty of hosts must demonstrate the sort of self-sacrificial love that engages even with those who may pose a threat to oneself, the very model of self-sacrificial love embodied by Jesus himself.

To make this case, this chapter will move in four steps. First, it offers a discussion of what the Bible says about migration, attending to the most relevant statements about the duties of both hosts and migrants. Second, there is a brief discussion of the critical points regarding what it means for a Christian to be a citizen, with particular focus on how the concept of Christians as dual citizens in this world impacts their role as hosts for migrants. Third, this material is synthesized into a view of what a Christian approach to integration comprises, before fourth and finally discussing a potential biblical example of this approach.

WHAT DOES THE BIBLE SAY ABOUT MIGRATION?

It is impossible to cover even the majority of topics one might discuss when thinking of the Bible and migration in the space available. A catalogue of the books of the Bible that either deal

---

5   Finding a robust answer to this question should be of importance to all. Yet, I would be remiss not to admit that it is acutely important to me since I am a migrant raising a family of migrant children in a foreign country.

explicitly with migration or are responses to that experience includes, in the Old Testament, Genesis, Exodus, Leviticus, Numbers, Deuteronomy, 1 Samuel, 1 and 2 Kings, 1 and 2 Chronicles, Ezra–Nehemiah, Isaiah, Jeremiah, Ezekiel, a large number of Psalms, Lamentations, Esther, and Daniel. From the New Testament, one can include Matthew, Acts of the Apostles, 1 Peter, Hebrews, and Revelation, with strong cases for a number of others too. One can justifiably describe the Bible as a collection of texts written by migrants to other migrants, often dealing with the issue of migration. To illustrate this feature, let us look briefly at the ancestral narrative in Genesis, some legal material from Exodus, Leviticus, and Deuteronomy, a key passage in the book of Jeremiah, the portrayal of Jesus as a migrant, and some New Testament statements about Christians as migrants.

Consider this unusual summary of the key figures in Genesis: Abraham, Isaac, and Jacob. Abraham migrates to Canaan from Mesopotamia (Genesis 12.1–10). Immediately upon arrival (Genesis 12.10), famine forces Abraham to flee to Egypt. To survive, Abraham instructs his wife Sarah to lie about their relationship. Predictably not well received by the Egyptians, this ruse still enables Abraham and Sarah to survive their time as refugees and to return to Canaan wealthier than they left. Abraham's son Isaac also faces famine (Genesis 26.1). Rather than leave Canaan, Isaac drifts about within Canaan, residing in various places to survive. Like father, like son: Isaac and his wife Rebekah employ the same tactic, hiding the true nature of their relationship. Their hosts are not pleased either, but, yet again, they emerge wealthier than they entered. Isaac's son Jacob grows up in Canaan, but spends 20 years seeking asylum with his family in Mesopotamia to avoid the aggression of his brother Esau (Genesis 27.41–28.9). While there, Jacob has to battle for his rights, because his Uncle Laban, despite providing him protection, holds immense power over him (Genesis 30.25–43). Just as with contemporary asylum seekers, Jacob treads carefully with Laban for fear that he might be returned to the dangerous situation he fled. Jacob finally gains his independence, and when he returns to Canaan, finds a transformed, unrecognizable society. Esau, who now seeks to reconcile with Jacob instead of killing him, exemplifies how much has changed in Jacob's absence (Genesis 33.1–17). Jacob goes through the experience of reverse culture shock, something familiar to anyone who has spent more than a few months away from home.

Throughout Genesis, these ancestors of Israel are referred to as *gēr*, a Hebrew term translated 'sojourner' or 'resident alien' that connotes transitory residence, difference from the host population, and limited legal protection. There are many ways this story corresponds to contemporary society. For instance, one can categorize Abraham, Isaac, and Jacob in terms used by the United Nations High Commissioner for Refugees: Abraham begins as a voluntary migrant, but then lives in Egypt as an environmentally induced, externally displaced person; Isaac is born to immigrant parents, and he subsequently becomes an environmentally induced, internally displaced person; Jacob is a third-generation migrant, who involuntarily migrates to seek asylum, before eventually repatriating by choice. All three figures are involuntary migrants.

It is no stretch to say that the traumatic experience of involuntary migration forms a core part of these stories, and therefore the identity of those who adopt it as a sacred text, like Christians. Genesis does not sugar-coat their experience either. Abraham, Isaac, and Jacob fear for their lives, behave in ways that trouble us, and sometimes must resort to questionable means to survive their precarious circumstances. A reader justifiably wonders if they are models of courage and resilience or if they are flawed characters who underscore our own shortcomings and moral failures. However one resolves that moral dilemma, it must not obscure that the ancestral narrative never advocates fear of outsiders. Nowhere is there a categorical resistance to engaging with those from another community. Genesis promotes engagement with outsiders and hospitality to others.

A distinct change of perspective occurs between Genesis and the legal material that follows it: whereas Genesis stresses the experience of those migrating, the legal texts focus far more extensively on the experience of hosting migrants.[6] To this end, two key terms for migrants in this material are *gēr* and *nokrî*.

---

6   There are, of course, the examples of Abraham as a short-term host (Genesis 18) and Laban hosting Jacob (Genesis 29–31). Still, these are exceptions to the widespread focus on the ancestors as migrants, not vice versa.

Nokrî designates a foreigner, likely one who has recently arrived and not integrated into the host community. The more frequent and more important term is *gēr* – usually translated as stranger or sojourner – which applies to a person of foreign origin who has assimilated into the host culture to some degree. For instance, the *gēr* celebrates the Sabbath along with Israel (e.g. Exodus 20.10). To underscore this level of integration, recall that Abraham and Jacob are both called *gēr*. This term even inspires the name of Moses' son Gershom, who is born as 'a stranger in a foreign land' (Exodus 18.3).

Uniquely in the ancient world, the legal texts often instruct the community to treat migrants as equals. For example, Leviticus commands the people to leave part of the harvest for 'the poor and the *gēr*' to gather (Leviticus 23.22). Moreover, Leviticus states: 'When a stranger (*gēr*) resides with you in your land, you shall not wrong him. The stranger who resides with you shall be to you as one of your citizens; you shall love him as yourself, for you were strangers in the land of Egypt' (Leviticus 19.33–34).

Exodus expresses a similar sentiment twice (Exodus 22.20, 23.9), with all three texts grounding this attitude in Israel's experience living as a *gēr* in Egypt. Perhaps it is no coincidence that instructions predicated on the experience in Egypt appear to match the openness towards foreigners advocated in Genesis. Of course, Leviticus and Exodus cast a vision for how this looks among the powerful host community, rather than in the minority immigrant group.

Despite advocating acceptance of some migrants, there are statements recommending caution towards them. Though Exodus calls for equal treatment of the *gēr*, elsewhere it excludes foreigners (*nokrî*) from the Passover (Exodus 12.43). Leviticus specifies that no animal from a foreigner can be sacrificed to God (Leviticus 22.25). Some texts even justify different treatment of the foreigner in the repayment of debts and in the loaning of money (Deuteronomy 15.3, 23.21). While these texts do allow for drawing distinctions between fellow citizen and foreigner – especially in religious practice – they do not in any way suggest the exclusion, rejection, or mistreatment of foreigners. It is possible these differing attitudes are related to distinctions between groups of migrants, with the *gēr* representing someone who has assimilated to the host culture more than the *nokrî*. These texts underscore that even in the ancient world dealing with migrants was no simple issue. And yet, they indicate that closed borders, negative rhetoric, and fearful responses do not characterize the people of God.

When one turns to the book of Jeremiah one finds a depiction of the events surrounding the final days prior to Jerusalem's destruction and the forced deportation of many of its inhabitants in 586 BCE. Jeremiah the prophet is not deported, but becomes an internally displaced involuntary migrant. That is, Jeremiah and his community are displaced within the borders of their country by an external force beyond their control. That experience differs from deportation to a foreign country, but it is hardly a continuation of life as normal. For comparison, consider those Syrians still residing within the borders of their war-ravaged country or the millions displaced within Colombia: though they have not crossed a border into another country, they most certainly are involuntary migrants.

It is hard to say in detail what life was like for those involuntary migrants from Jerusalem taken to the city of Babylon. There is anecdotal evidence that they had some freedom about where they settled in Babylon, a city that must have struck them as vast and strangely cosmopolitan relative to Jerusalem. The book of Jeremiah indicates these former residents of Jerusalem lived among the Babylonians. Indeed, it strongly encourages them to engage openly with their hosts:

> Thus said the LORD of Hosts, the God of Israel, to the whole community which I exiled from Jerusalem to Babylon: Build houses and live in them, plant gardens and eat their fruit. Take wives and beget sons and daughters; and take wives for your sons, and give your daughters to husbands, that they may bear sons and daughters. Multiply there, do not decrease. And seek the welfare of the city to which I have exiled you and pray to the LORD in its behalf; for in its prosperity you shall prosper. (Jeremiah 29.4–7)

Contemporary research on migrants indicates that this sort of pragmatic, accommodating attitude is common among migrants with some choice about where they live or those who live in close proximity to outsiders.[7] Jeremiah implies that these deportees from Jerusalem lived in a multicultural, integrated setting that promoted an open attitude towards foreign communities.

Whereas Jeremiah depicts a community of migrants with some control over where they lived, the book of Ezekiel recalls something else entirely. Ezekiel addresses essentially the same period as Jeremiah – the destruction of Jerusalem and the forced deportations in its aftermath. However, Ezekiel does not address a community in Babylon living among other groups, but one placed in a remote area, probably in a work camp meant to build a canal. Formerly the elite of Jerusalem, these men and women became manual labourers forced to work for the imperial power that destroyed their city. Ezekiel's response is to draw hard lines between its community and anyone seen as an outsider, even fellow Jerusalemites who it thinks disagrees with him. The strongly insular, ethnocentric response is characteristic of many contemporary involuntary migrants settled in refugee camps. Though the ancient and modern settings do have substantial differences one should not discount, the comparison intimates that using camps or other living arrangements that isolate migrant groups from the host community may work directly against the ideal of integrating groups across enduring lines of difference.

Moving to the New Testament, it is now familiar for people to say 'Jesus was a refugee'. This statement focuses on the depiction of the holy family fleeing Herod's aggression by seeking safety in Egypt (Matthew 2.13–15). It is crucial to note that in this passage the Gospel of Matthew emphasizes that Jesus shares the experiences of Israel.[8] The main point is that Jesus doesn't just sympathize with the involuntary migrants that feature throughout the Old Testament, but he can draw on his own life experience to empathize with them. Jesus exemplifies empathy for the displaced and marginalized, suggesting that the Christian call to be conformed to Christ must include this feature to some degree as well.

---

7   For instance, Colson, E. (2003) 'Forced migration and the anthropological response', pp.7–8. *Journal of Refugee Studies 16,* 1.
8   For further background on this passage, see Bockmuehl, M. (1994) *This Jesus,* pp.34–36. London: T. & T. Clark.

Rather more needs to be added to this rhetoric about Jesus as refugee. There are further, important, similarities between Jesus and another category of migrants: Roma, or gypsies as they are sometimes known. Defined as 'a member of a traditionally itinerant people living by itinerant trade', the Roma evoke much of what we know about Jesus of Nazareth. He was a man who travelled from town to town, living on the support of people who valued his teaching, even declaring that, 'foxes have holes, and birds of the air have nests; but the Son of Man [Jesus' way of referencing himself] has nowhere to lay his head' (Matthew 8.20; see also Luke 9.58). It is true that the 'itinerant' religious leader is a well-attested figure in antiquity, and one who enjoyed cultural acceptance in ancient Judaism. Still, it is notable that Jesus of Nazareth's lifestyle resembles the perennial movements and cultural marginalization so common among the Roma instead of a settled lifestyle common among those empowered to make judgments about how to treat them.

Lest it slip away, the main point remains that the central figure of Christianity lived as a marginal, mobile person, mixing frequently and openly with so-called outsiders. Some of those outsiders – the Roman centurion and the tax collectors representing Rome, for instance – represented clear and present dangers to the survival of all that Jesus' own community revered. Still, no group was more hated by Jesus' community than the Samaritans.

Closely related to the Jewish community that focused its religious life on Jerusalem, the Samaritans worshipped the same God in Samaria. To those loyal to Jerusalem, this was a heinous perversion of their beliefs and practices. More than any other 'enemy', the Samaritans represented a threat residing just on the other side of a 'porous' border. How did Jesus handle this situation? To begin, he did not avoid Samaria; according to the Gospel of John, Jesus travelled through Samaria, voluntarily stopping in one of its towns to converse with a woman of 'ill repute' and to stay for two days among its people (John 4.1–42). Furthermore, when Jesus had to explain the greatest commandments of Judaism – to love the Lord your God with all your heart and your neighbour as yourself (Luke 10.27) – he selected a Samaritan as his paradigmatic example of faithfulness.

The Parable of the Good Samaritan is so familiar that the story has lost some of its most radical features. Astonishing as it would have been to Jesus' audience that the Samaritan helped the man from Jerusalem, it would have pushed the bounds of believability to imagine that Samaritan taking the injured man to the inn where he leaves this Jerusalemite to recover (Luke 10.34–35). Why? Well, what would those Jews think was the cause of this Jewish man's injuries: bad luck or the hated Samaritan who brought his badly injured body into the building? The parable describes an ancient equivalent to a gang member carrying an injured member of his rival gang into a public place where his rivals congregate. This parable seeks to underscore not just that the Samaritan helps someone unlike him, but goes so far as to place himself in imminent danger to ensure the injured man finds safe haven. The parable summons us to love those people – especially those people – who we think threaten our community.

Rabbi Lord Jonathan Sacks, writing on this command to love, observes that:

> The Hebrew Bible contains the great command, 'You shall love your neighbour as yourself' (Leviticus 19.18), and this has often been taken as the basis of biblical morality. But it is not: it is only part of it. The Jewish sages noted that on only one occasion does the Hebrew Bible command us to love our neighbour, but in thirty-seven places it commands us to love the stranger.[9]

Jewish and Christian traditions both go to great lengths to teach the necessity of providing care to those outside the community who, in very many cases, present a threat to that which one's own community holds sacred.

Other passages in the New Testament reinforce this perspective by defining the Christian community as a whole in migratory terms. The letter called 1 Peter opens by referring to its audience, a collection of Christian groups in Asia Minor, as exiles or refugees (*parepidemos*). This manner of address indicates that the earliest Christian communities understood themselves in this way, or at least regarded it as a reasonable metaphor for their experience. Similarly, Hebrews 11 describes its paragons of

---

9   Sacks, J. (1997) *Faith in the Future*, p.78. Macon, GA: Mercer University Press.

faith by recalling that they 'confess that they were strangers and foreigners on the earth' (Hebrews 11.13).

This overview, albeit brief, shows that the Bible speaks extensively about migration. In most cases, the texts speak from the perspective of the migrant, even characterizing a Christian life by analogy to this experience. There are places – the legal material of the Old Testament and Jesus' re-presentation of these ideas in his parables – that address the role of host community. What it means to be a Christian host needs further attention.

CHRISTIANS AS DUAL CITIZENS

In addition to the discussion of biblical texts on being a host, it is necessary to consider and take account of what the New Testament says about Christians as citizens, not just of nation-states, but also of the kingdom of God.

Nigel Biggar addresses the question of Christianity and patriotism in Chapter 2, offering a useful description of citizenship. 'It is proper for an individual to have affection for, feel loyalty to, and show gratitude toward those communities that have enabled her to flourish',[10] argues Biggar. One might complement that explanation with the concept of allegiance. For instance, the United States stresses this concept by having school children regularly recite a 'pledge of allegiance'. Though allegiance is not a common way to describe Christian faith, it is an accurate account. To confess that Jesus is Lord means to assert allegiance to a Messiah – an anointed king – who claims dominion over all aspects of life. The ultimate allegiance of Christians to Jesus' kingdom moderates Christian allegiance to a nation-state in important ways. Biggar argues that, even where national loyalty is fitting, it should be limited,[11] explaining that when loyalty to the nation would require harm to the community, true fidelity requires one to refuse such actions. 'True patriotism is not uncritical', affirms Biggar, who further maintains that, 'in extreme circumstances true patriotism might even involve participation in acts of treason'.[12]

---

10 See page 49.
11 See Chapter 2.
12 See page 58.

Explorations of citizenship generally appeal to Philippians 3.20, which identifies Christians as citizens of heaven to encourage its audience to endure faithfully in the face of persecution and trials. That is not irrelevant here, but tangential. More pertinent are the analogies in 1 Peter 1 and Hebrews 11 and, even less frequently raised in this domain, the Johannine concept that followers of Jesus 'do not belong to the world' (John 17.16) even though they are not to escape from it.

The relationship of these various ideas to citizenship and the obligations a Christian bears as a citizen of an earthly nation-state are encapsulated succinctly and powerfully in the second-century CE Epistle to Diognetus. 'Christians', it remarks, 'are indistinguishable from other [people] either by nationality, language or customs':

> they do not inhabit separate cities of their own, or speak a strange dialect, or follow some outlandish way of life. ...And yet there is something extraordinary about their lives. They live in their own countries as though they were only passing through. They play their full role as citizens, but labor under all the disabilities of aliens. Any country can be their homeland, but for them their homeland, wherever it may be, is a foreign country.[13]

Christians, this passage eloquently articulates, live as citizens, but as citizens who are radically committed to identifying with migrants. While followers of Jesus 'play their full role as citizens', they possess the capability to identify and empathize with someone who finds themself dealing with the challenges of not residing in their native home.

In short, the very nature of Christian identity necessitates straddling lines of enduring difference and integrating into an unfamiliar and essentially temporary home. The New Testament outlines a way of living as a citizen that demands identifying with the migrant. This creates tension, no doubt, but also enables the Christian to inhabit a unique role in the process of integrating newcomers into a community.

---

13   www.vatican.va/spirit/documents/spirit_20010522_diogneto_en.html. For a critical edition of the text, see Jefford, C.N. (2013) *The Epistle to Diognetus (with the Fragment of Quadratus)*. Oxford: Oxford University Press.

Thanks to C.B. Hays for pointing me to this quotation.

A CHRISTIAN APPROACH TO INTEGRATION: MUTUAL OBLIGATION

It is now possible to synthesize the biblical material on hosts, migrants, and citizenship in order to outline a Christian vision for how hosts and migrants should engage with one another. That vision advocates mutually beneficial integration that does not eliminate important aspects of difference among individuals or groups, based upon obligations for hosts and migrants.

The legal material of the Old Testament repeatedly commands the people of God to live as a host society that loves the stranger (Leviticus 19.10, 19.33–34, 23.22, 24.22; Numbers 9.14, 15.14–15; Deuteronomy 10.18, 14.29, 24.17, 24.19–21, 26.12–13, 27.19). Though not all migrants receive the same treatment (i.e. *gēr* and *nokrî*), the texts are clear that hosts should always assume a posture of welcome. Crucially, the Old Testament instructs the community to adopt behaviours that provide a safety net of material care for the immigrant should they not be able to provide for themselves (e.g. Leviticus 23.22). That duty not only recurs in the New Testament, but the parable of the Good Samaritan expands it to encompass caring for even a despised outsider when doing so may endanger one's own wellbeing. Hosts, in a Christian understanding of them, should not expect immigrants to give up or compromise their identity, but seek to love and serve them, across enduring lines of difference that may cause suspicion and fear. This is a hard saying, but that does not prevent it from being a Christian obligation (John 6.60–69).

These radical obligations for hosts do not stand alone, but rather in mutual reinforcement with the duty of migrants to seek the welfare of their host community. This concept is most clearly enunciated in Jeremiah 29, the letter to the exiles in Babylon. Recall that this passage directs those people forcibly deported from Jerusalem and settled in Babylon to settle into their new environment, to seek the welfare (*shalom*) of that city and to pray for its flourishing.

Shalom or welfare does not simply include economic prosperity or the absence of violence; it envisions a comprehensive flourishing. Cornelius Plantinga encapsulates this complex notion well in his statement that *shalom* is 'the webbing together of God, humans, and all creation in justice, fulfilment, and delight'.[14] Migrants, wherever they find themselves and for whatever reason – within or beyond their control – are called by God to behave in a way that promotes cohesion, personal and communal wellbeing, and contributes to an environment in which all people can experience joy.

When Jeremiah 29 suggests this form of engagement by migrants with foreign populations, it does not advocate giving up one's identity. Indeed, the passage subsequently envisions a time when this migrant community will return to its ancestral land (Jeremiah 29.14). Still, migrants are called to seek the welfare of the communities in which they live, though not to abandon their uniqueness, their customs, or other enduring lines of difference, so long as these things do not preclude love for others as fellow humans made in the image of God – an obligation Christians believe applies in all times and places. Migrants, instead, should embrace a new culture and a new set of neighbours across difference. Or, as expressed in John 17, migrants are not required to abandon their identity to become undifferentiated members of the society in which they live, but they are called to live in a way that does not seek to avoid interaction with that society.

THE EPISTLE TO THE ROMANS: A CHRISTIAN MANIFESTO ABOUT INTEGRATION?

One place where one may find these ideas applied in the New Testament is Paul's Epistle to the Romans. For those familiar with Romans, that may seem an odd notion. Evidence nevertheless suggests that Romans addressed the aftermath of Roman emperor Claudius expelling Jews thought to be causing disturbances in Rome, some of whom were connected to the Christian Church there.[15] It is possible that Paul wrote this letter to guide the Roman church in dealing with the return of its Jewish members who were forcibly removed some time ago. The Jewish Christians

---

14   Plantinga Jr., C. (1995) *Not the Way It's Supposed to Be: A Breviary of Sin*, p.10. Grand Rapids, MI: Eerdmans.

15   For discussion of the issue, see Wright, N.T. (2002) 'The Letter to the Romans: Introduction, Commentary, and Reflections.' In *The New Interpreters Bible, Vol. X.* Nashville, TN: Abingdon, especially pp.406–448.

were not unknown to the community, but, returning after a long absence, for all intents and purposes they were unfamiliar immigrants. Taken in this context, Paul discusses how to deal with a sudden surge in immigration that will substantially impact the community.

Paul's statements about the shared experience of Jews and Gentiles exhibits new relevance from this perspective. To underscore that 'all, both Jews and Greeks, are under the power of sin' (Romans 3.9) and that God is the God of Jews and Gentiles together (Romans 3.29) emphasizes the similarities that exist between host community and immigrants despite enduring lines of difference between them. Paul marvels that anyone would 'pass judgment on your brother or sister' (Romans 14.10; see also Romans 11.17–24), for 'each of us will be accountable to God' (Romans 14.12). He instructs them to 'no longer pass judgment on one another, but resolve instead never to put a stumbling block or hindrance in the way of another' (Romans 14.13). Speaking most broadly, Paul implores the church at Rome to 'welcome one another, therefore, just as Christ has welcomed you' (Romans 15.7). Rephrased in terms concerned with migration and integration, Paul's guidance to the Gentile community in Rome and to the Jewish community returning there is to engage with one another in obedience to the obligations God has placed upon them. The Gentile community – the host group – is not to think of themselves as better than the migrants. In fact, as Christian citizens, God calls this community to identify with these migrants, to assume a posture of welcome towards them, and to show them hospitality when they return to Rome (Romans 12.13). The Jewish migrants coming back to Rome, likewise, are not to remain separate from the Gentiles, not to seek to establish a community of their own in Rome, not to escape from that world. Rather, Paul casts a vision for an embrace between two groups across the lines of difference in culture and experience that separate them. Indeed, the Jewish returnees should look for ways to help construct a community in which everyone might have the opportunity to flourish.

This remains a hypothetical reading of Romans on the available evidence. And yet, it is an illuminating one that challenges the reader to reflect upon integration in a fresh way – whether one is the host, migrant, or observer.

CONCLUSIONS: EMBRACING OTHERS ACROSS ENDURING LINES OF DIFFERENCE

This chapter has argued that the biblical material concerning migration in the Old and New Testaments supports a Christian view of citizenship, migration, and integration that is not primarily interested in the rights of any party or in determining what any group might be entitled to receive. The guiding principle for the Christian – supported by the range of material from both Old and New Testaments – involves obligations God places upon hosts and migrants. Old and New Testament texts instruct hosts to empathize with the migrant and to self-sacrificially serve them. Migrants, for their part, should behave in a way that promotes cohesion with the host and the wellbeing of all. Integration that results in the flourishing of all requires hosts and migrants to embrace one another across their differences in this sort of mutually beneficial way.

How then should Christians residing in host communities – whether that be in the United Kingdom or elsewhere – respond to the present increase in migration and its accompanying challenges to successful integration of new arrivals? What, in other words, would one do if they accepted this understanding of the biblical material on migration and integration?

It is impossible to answer that question comprehensively, though a few actionable responses can be highlighted. These actions relate to one another in concentric circles, moving from a small, local context, to successively larger national and international settings.

The central circle comprises the local church, where Jesus instructs Christians to incarnate the vision of a properly functioning community for the rest of the world to see. As an immediate, practical, and tangible step, Christians might proactively find ways to build community across the enduring lines of difference that exist among Christian hosts and migrants in a single city. A simple strategy would be to create opportunities to eat together – both the liturgical, Eucharistic meal, but also informal, non-liturgical meals – with Christian migrants that live in one's locality. Invoking shared faith and employing the shared Eucharistic meal as a foundation, this strategy offers an opportunity for all involved to work out the challenges of embracing another across an enduring line of difference in a context where grace, mercy, and patience should be readily in supply. This strategy is hardly innovative: St Paul's letter to the church in Galatia calls for this very practice (Galatians 2.11–21).

Expanding out from this horizon, these mutually caring Christian communities might look for ways to engage a wider, non-Christian community of migrants in a form of self-sacrificial love. Perhaps this takes the form of another meal, perhaps the form of a food bank that provides for people seeking asylum who are not able to work (a contemporary form of the command in Leviticus 23.22), or perhaps something entirely different altogether. Ultimately, each local community will need to identify the most relevant and helpful way that it can begin to fulfil its obligation as a host, irrespective of whether the migrant community understands or commits to seeking the welfare of their host. This final matter is of crucial importance: the obligation of hosts to care for migrants exists regardless of whether the migrant recognizes their corresponding duty to seek the welfare of their host. To respond in this way represents faithfulness to the demand articulated in the parable of the Good Samaritan.

Most broadly, at the national and international level, Christians should approach these undeniably complex and challenging issues surrounding migration and integration with a particularly Christian vision of citizenship in mind. Recalling that Christians should 'play their full role as citizens, but labour under all the disabilities of aliens',[16] followers of Jesus bear a responsibility to engage with policy makers and non-governmental organizations in a way that demonstrates their effort to identify and empathize with migrants. Policy proposals, responses by national governments, the activities of international political bodies, and the work of non-governmental groups should all be evaluated against the twin obligations of the host both to employ their resources to care for the stranger and also to speak on their behalf, especially when they have a limited ability to do so themselves. Christians can and should evaluate whether or not the financial, political, cultural, and relational capital deployed by

16   www.vatican.va/spirit/documents/spirit_20010522_diogneto_en.html.

their national government and other institutions in which they have a stake aligns with these commitments.

By all means, Christians should support policies and initiatives that encourage migrants to contribute to the cohesion of their communities and to create an environment that is ever more conducive to the flourishing of all residents (i.e. Jeremiah 29). Precisely what form such initiatives and programmes might take is admittedly hard to know, but that lack of clarity does not eradicate the requirement to encourage such responses.

A robust, thoughtful, and faithful response to the issues surrounding migration and integration will be no less complex than those issues themselves. This exploration reflects that reality. The approach outlined here no doubt has shortcomings in its details and will find resistance in some of its parts; such is always the case. Be that as it may, it foregrounds guiding principles that can and should guide the attitudes of and responses by people on all sides of this issue. The hope remains that engaging with the difficult questions about integration in this way will better equip Christians to serve others and to live as citizens of their respective countries in a way that prompts people to marvel, 'and yet there is something extraordinary about their lives'.[17]

---

17   www.vatican.va/spirit/documents/spirit_20010522_diogneto_en.html.

Chapter Six

CITIZENS, MIGRANTS AND STATES

Ben Ryan, London, UK

INTRODUCTION

Citizenship is a matter of belonging. Those who are citizens are members of a community and, as a result of their citizenship, are entitled to particular rights and status. In the modern world citizenship is something granted by states. The British Prime Minister, Theresa May, encapsulated this issue in a speech to the Conservative Party conference in 2016 in which she declared that, 'if you believe you're a citizen of the world, you're a citizen of nowhere'.[1]

She was, in a sense, perfectly correct. Citizenship, and more broadly, all political and civic identity, is seen as coterminous with the borders of the state. Citizenship is, accordingly, intimately tied up with debates over the notion of a nation-state – a bounded homogeneous community. Within that context migration is particularly important. It is in relation to the rights of migrants that citizenship most clearly comes into the public policy arena, and it is in relation to migrants that debates over the cohesiveness of society are most fiercely contested.

A Christian contribution to citizenship needs to establish the underpinning values and moral basis to that debate. At present, the rationale behind state approaches to citizenship has become entirely focused on the interests of states over individuals. Economic demands, security and a demand for assimilation have overtaken other factors.

---

1   Theresa May, Keynote speech to the Conservative Party conference, Birmingham, 5 October 2016.

Making a Christian case is to challenge that development, and the basis of a citizenship based on a 'methodological nationalism',[2] which sees political identity as subsisting wholly within the borders of the nation-state. Only by challenging that model can a Christian vision of citizenship for a new age begin to be built on the basis of rights, responsibilities and human dignity over and above the interests of states.

This chapter will explore how the current status quo has formed, with state interests and fears over a loss of homogeneity taking preference over other factors. It will then propose the building blocks for a Christian conception of citizenship that start from the principle of human dignity and the need for a rights-based approach.

THE STATE WE'RE IN

There is an irony to the fact that the state model which proves such a difficulty for Christians in the Middle East is itself a product of fratricidal Christian conflict. The Peace of Westphalia in 1648 which brought about the end of the Thirty-Years War is widely considered to mark the origin of the idea of a nation-state. The nation, the prototype for which is the Israel of the Old Testament, is a people connected by a shared ethnicity (and then, though latterly less so, by a shared religion). The state, by contrast, is not ethnic, but refers to an organized, bounded, political community. When combined into the nation-state it produces the idea of a bounded, homogeneous community under a single government.

This new unit of politics, the nation-state, provided a pragmatic solution to the wars of the Early Modern period. Henceforth, territories would be marked by clear borders, under defined separate government, within which there would be (at least theoretically) a single homogenized community defined in Westphalia, and other Early Modern treaties, by a shared religion. The famous line *cuius regio, eius religio* (Whose realm, his religion) was coined at the Peace of Augsburg in 1555, reflecting this new reality. The very word 'state' which was previously little

---

2   Zaman, T. (2017) 'A Right to Neighbourhood: Rethinking Islamic Narratives and Practices of Hospitality in a Sedentarist World.' In L. Mavelli and E. Wilson (eds) *The Refugee Crisis and Religion*. London: Rowman & Littlefield.

used began to become mainstream, replacing previous common terminology like 'commonwealth' as the title of a distinct political territory.[3] There is an irony that the Protestant reformation which did so much to create a sense of the individual[4] also served as a catalyst for the creation of an all-encompassing homogenizing force in the form of the nation-state.

This conception of a political unit which is clearly bounded (with borders that can be drawn on a map within which there is a single political authority), and which is made up of a linked and homogeneous community within those borders has lasted ever since. Its continuing power is visible in many settings, but one clear one is the so-called 'two state solution' as a means of resolving the Palestine–Israel conflict. The proposed solution, give or take much negotiation, is to have two separate bounded homogeneous communities, one made up of Israelis and one of Palestinians.

Nor, despite some expectations to the contrary over the past 20 years, is this model declining. At the time of the 1994 Maastricht Treaty that brought in European citizenship, many were speculating that we might be seeing the end of the nation-state.[5] The past few years have demonstrated the naivety of that belief. Worldwide, the importance of control of national borders, the sense of threat to the community and nation are on the increase.

The concept of the border has become a major political concern. Globalization, the media and the advances in transportation have, perhaps paradoxically, only increased and emphasized the importance of borders and local identity.[6] These developments have caused pressure to be placed on the model of the nation-state, to which nation-states have been forced to respond, often in ways that have undermined Christian values. It is to those responses that this chapter now turns.

---

3   Greengrass, M. (2013) *Christendom Destroyed: Europe 1517–1648*. St Ives: Penguin.
4   See, for example, Ryrie, C.C. (2017) *Protestants: The Faith that Made the Modern World*. London: Penguin and Siedentop, L. (2014) *Inventing the Individual: The Origins of Western Liberalism*. Cambridge, MA: Harvard University Press.
5   For example, Ohmae, K. (1995) *The End of the Nation State: The Rise of Regional Economies*. New York, NY: Simon & Schuster.
6   Snyder, S. (2011) 'Globalization: Challenges to Christianity.' *Journal of World Christianity 4*, 1, 44–54.

MODERNITY AS A THREAT TO THE NATION-STATE

The nation-state has two defining features. The first is that it is a bounded community, with borders within which the government is sovereign. The second is that it contains, in theory if not always in practice, a homogeneous national community. If either of those features is threatened, the nation-state as a whole is threatened. The modern world radically challenges both features in three particular ways.

1. The nation-state is undermined if there is a breakdown in its internal homogeneity

This is a fear of many of the world's current nation-states – that their national identity is being somehow eroded. Perhaps their particular defining characteristic is in decline. For example, the Westphalian peace, as we have seen, defined the nation-state by the faith of its ruler – Protestant or Catholic. Such distinctions lose meaning if the faith content of that identity declines – as it has done across the West.[7]

Alternatively, other essential values or identity markers may have fallen by the wayside. Institutions are one such example. The military often plays a key symbolic role as an institutional embodiment of the nation-state, and where its prestige is deemed to be in decline, so too, therefore, is the nation itself. A common fear is that individualism has undermined faith and loyalty to institutions to the extent that the internal homogeneity of the state itself comes under threat.[8]

This threat to an undermining of internal homogeneity is all the more emphasized in states in which that homogeneity was always, in fact, rather strained, or even fictional. In practice, there are few true nation-states anywhere which genuinely embody a single homogeneous community with a shared language, history, religion and values.

This is especially the case in the Middle East context. In many states across the Middle East the extent of heterogeneity

---

7   Fox, J. (2013) *An Introduction to Religion and Politics: Theory and Practice.* Oxford: Routledge.
8   Sutherland, P.D. (2008) 'A golden mean between multiculturalism and assimilation.' *Studies: An Irish Quarterly Review 97,* 385, 73–86.

in religion, ethnicity and language is quite remarkable. Lebanon, for example has a minority Christian population that accounts for up to 40 per cent of the total,[9] as well as a population of the Druze whose numbers in surveys vary wildly (perhaps because they are sometimes classified as an Islamic sect). Under strain, as we shall see, states across the Middle East have clamped down on this internal heterogeneity. The net result of this is the near elimination of many minority religious groups across the region. Among those to have come under particular strain are the Druze, Yazidis and Mandaeans.[10] Christianity is one religion among several which was born in the Middle East and may soon be eliminated from the region entirely.

2. The nation-state is undermined if its internal homogeneity is undermined by the arrival of outsiders

Alongside the fear of an internal breakdown in homogeneity is a fear of pressure on homogeneity posed by migration. It is worth stressing again that many Christians are not migrants but have always been in place within the Middle East. There is, however, a not insignificant Christian foreign-born population in many Middle East states. There is a long history, for example, of Filipino labourers particularly in Saudi Arabia and other oil-producing states.[11]

More broadly we live in a context in which there is now an astonishing level of migration, including many Christian migrants. Worldwide there are an estimated 244 million migrants including 20 million refugees.[12] Whether in the Middle East or elsewhere, there is a visceral fear that the arrival of so many people from different cultures radically undermines the internal homogeneity

---

9   Pew Research Centre, Religion and Public Life (2015) 'The Future of World Religions: Population Growth Projections, 2010–2050.' Available at www.pewforum.org/2015/04/02/religious-projections-2010-2050, accessed on 22 March 2017.

10   Russell, G. (2014) *Heirs to Forgotten Kingdoms: Journeys into the Disappearing Religions of the Middle East.* London: Simon & Schuster.

11   Parthasarathi, P. and Quayaert, D. (2011) 'Migrant workers in the Middle East: Introduction'. *International Labor and Working-Class History 79*, 1, 4–6.

12   UN DESA (2015) *International Migration Report 2015.* Available at www.un.org/en/development/desa/population/migration/publications/migrationreport/docs/MigrationReport2015.pdf, accessed on 22 March 2017.

of the nation-state. This cannot be simply dismissed as racism. There is evidence that different migrant communities do indeed settle and integrate with different levels of success in different cultures at different times.[13]

3. The bounded nature of a nation-state can be challenged by external agents

The most obvious example of this is by military intervention by a foreign force. In the Middle East, the rise of the Islamic State and the extent of international intervention are the most prominent examples of state borders being challenged by external agents. Aside from military challenges to borders there are also several other aspects by which it is perceived that the bounded nature of states comes under threat.

For example, the nature of global economics today is such that, in practice, the ability of some states to operate is limited by the global market. Capital flows between states can undermine national policies, while tax arrangements and havens prevent national governments from controlling tax returns from companies operating within their borders. In the case of those Middle East states receiving international aid from abroad there are also contractual relationships that limit the freedom of those states to operate. International bodies, of which the EU is the most prominent example, also present a means by which states can surrender sovereignty in exchange for some (usually economic) gain.

These external threats, while important, sit beyond the scope of this essay.

STATE RESPONSES TO THE CHALLENGES TO HOMOGENEITY

In response to the challenges outlined above nation-states have adopted a number of tactics to protect themselves. The most common four have been multiculturalism, the adoption of the

---

13   Maxwell, R. (2010) 'Evaluating migrant integration: Political attitudes across generations in Europe.' *The International Migration Review 44*, 1, 25–52.

market state, assimilation and securitization. Each of these four tactics raises particular challenges for Christians.

1. Multiculturalism

Multiculturalism can of course be nothing more than a normative sociological description. As a political ideology, it has not always received a generous press. It was adopted by the Canadian government of Pierre Trudeau in the 1970s and 1980s and the UK government of Tony Blair in the late 1990s and early 2000s. It is often characterized as a policy designed to let all cultures and faiths live alongside one another without any efforts at assimilation, though that is to over-generalize what was proposed in both Canada and the UK.

Fair or not, the accusation that this policy failed to meaningfully build national loyalty among minority and migrant groups has led to it largely being abandoned. It was perceived as creating a ghettoization of communities that was never going to be conducive to the promotion of the common good or meaningful integration. At its worst, it falls into a classic liberal trap, which is to mistake tolerance for love. This was a point made by the Catholic priest Tomas Halik in a lecture in 2014 on receiving the Templeton Prize. Halik noted that Jesus' astonishing command to love your neighbour demanded more than accepting them and leaving them to their own devices. Meaningful community requires more than acceptance, it demands some genuine encounter. It is for this reason that this particular solution falls short of a truly Christian vision of citizenship. At any rate, it is no longer a sufficiently common policy choice as to merit much attention.

2. The market state

A second tactic adopted by states has been to, in effect, sideline the issue of internal homogeneity by instead recasting the nation-state as the market state. In this scenario, cultural and societal markers are downplayed in favour of a purely economic assessment of human worth. This has been particularly used as the tactic for dealing with migrants, who are accepted or rejected based purely on their ability to contribute to the national economy.

In the case of some migration policies (most notably Australia), this is formalized into a quota system that admits migrants to the country primarily on the basis of whether they meet particular labour market needs.

It also applies to the granting of citizenship towards people born abroad. Several Middle Eastern states have historically encouraged a certain degree of labour movement. In fact, compared with Western Europe, the Middle East has seen significantly higher labour migration. By the early 1980s foreign workers made up 70 per cent of Kuwait's workforce, 81 per cent of Qatar's, 40 per cent of Bahrain's, 85 per cent of the UAE's and 75 per cent of Saudi Arabia's.[14] Jordan was forced in that period to import foreign workers in order to replace those Jordanians who had gone to work in its oil-producing neighbours. This scale of labour did not lend itself to states desiring to grant residency rights or citizenship. In fact, the opposite occurred; there was no desire to expand their citizenship to cover this vast number of foreigners.

This is probably one explanation for the fact that Middle Eastern states are among the toughest in which to gain citizenship. In several, including Dubai, there is no means by which a foreign-born individual can apply for citizenship, while in others citizenship is only very rarely granted. This causes a number of abuses. Since these workers are not citizens, their rights and status are not protected by the state in which they work, but their own state. The ability of their own state to lobby for and protect the rights of workers is limited. In the case of the several million foreign workers in Saudi Arabia, there has been a tendency for states to be more concerned with maintaining good diplomatic relationships and the ability to continue to export labour (in the case of some, like the Philippines, a key asset to their own economy) than to protect workers overseas.

There are several other reasons to resist this approach to migration and citizenship, both from Christian and secular perspectives. One is that such a policy has been shown time and again to cause resentment, as native workers feel undermined.

14   Humphrey, M. (1993) 'Migrants, workers and refugees: The political economy of population movements in the Middle East.' *Middle East Report 181*, Radical Movements: Migrants, Workers and Refugees, 2–7.

This is both bad for social cohesion and makes such workers a target for potential abuse.

For Christians, a broader concern might be that this policy de-humanizes migrants. People are turned into nothing more than commodified labour, valued only in so far as they contribute to the economic machine. This is reflected throughout in migrant policies that are defined purely in terms of interests. The interests of the state, employers and the labour market come to dominate discourse on migrant policy.[15] Notable in this is that migration policies rarely, if ever, seem to reflect the interests of individual migrants. This perpetuates a de-humanized vision of migrants, or in the words of Pope Francis:

> The prevailing mentality puts the flow of people at the service of the flow of capital, resulting in many cases in the exploitation of employees as if they were objects to be used, discarded and thrown out.[16]

There is also a sense in which this prioritizes a very particular conception of labour, namely what eighteenth-century economists like Adam Smith would have termed 'productive labour'. Productive labour is that which contributes to the wealth of society at large. There is certainly a Biblical warrant for the necessity and dignity of work. Even before the Fall, humanity is created with the expectation that they will till the ground (Genesis 2.5) and cultivate and care for Eden (Genesis 2.15). Jesus in the parable of the Talents (Matthew 25.14–30) admonishes the lazy servant who buries what he is given rather than working hard to get his master a return. In his second letter to the Thessalonians, Paul famously advises them that if one of them is unwilling to work he should not eat (2 Thessalonians 3.10).

However, this does not mean that the biblical warrant for the value of work is reduced to the idea of delivering maximal wealth into the economy. Indeed, the importance of the Sabbath, a day of rest, emphasizes above all else that work is not the full and only

---

15   Battistella, R.G. (2008) 'Migration and Human Dignity: From Policies of Exclusion to Policies Based on Human Rights.' In D.G. Groody and G. Campese (eds) *A Promised Land, A Perilous Journey: Theological Perspectives on Migration.* Notre Dame, IN: University of Notre Dame Press.

16   Pope Francis (2016) 'Meeting with World of Labour.' Speech delivered at Bachilleres College, State of Chihuahua, Ciudad Juárez. 17 February.

purpose of humanity. Whether or not it is maximally beneficial to the economy, God calls for humans to rest. Nor is the compulsion to work divorced from a respect for labour rights – not only rest, but fair pay, with Jesus declaring that 'the labourer deserves his payment' (Luke 10.7). Most fundamentally, while work is important, it is not to be understood simply as commodified labour. The importance of caring for the sick, the elderly, children, family members, these are just a few examples of immensely important work that contributes towards the common good, but which has little economic value within these assessments.

The market state model, therefore, seems some way short of the optimal Christian principle for assessing citizenship or migration policy.

3. Assimilation

Promoting integration by assimilation is a policy that seems to be growing in popularity across the globe. A glance at the development of citizenship tests in countries like the USA and the UK, for example, shows that such tests are becoming more difficult and demand greater levels of assimilation than ever before. Compulsory language classes for migrants are a policy that has grown over recent years. A Council of Europe report found that, in 2010, 23 states (of the 31 that responded to the survey) made language knowledge a requirement for admission to the country, permanent residence or acquisition of citizenship.[17]

Languages are a soft aspect of assimilation. Harder asks include the demands for oaths of allegiance – despite the fact that the evidence for the success of these in promoting integration is limited[18] – or in particular demands about dress, religious observance, and cultural behaviours. In the West, such debates have tended to particularly revolve around a perceived problem with Islam. Bans on particular items of clothing, such as the Hijab, are one such example.

---

17   Extramiana, C. and Van Avermaet, P. (2011) 'Language requirements for adult migrants in Council of Europe member states: Report on a survey.' Strasbourg: Council of Europe, Language Policy Division.

18   See El-Haj, A. (2009) 'Becoming citizens in an era of globalization and transnational migration: Re-imagining citizenship as critical practice.' *Theory into Practice 48*, 4, 274–282 and Maxwell (2010).

However, while the West has its weaknesses in this regard, it is fair to say that things are much worse across the Middle East. Jonathan Fox has identified 30 separate types of religious discrimination used by states.[19] These discriminatory policies tend to be used to enforce the homogeneity of the in-group by undermining minority groups. In Fox's study, he looks at the treatment of Muslims in 26 Western democracies, and the treatment of Christians in 17 Middle Eastern Muslim-majority states.

He concludes that while policies against Muslims appear to be on the rise, with 16 of the 30 types of religious discrimination present in at least one Western democracy, nonetheless the discrimination does not tend to be overly systematic. Only three of these restrictions appear in more than two or three Western states. By contrast, 28 types of discrimination were tracked against Christians in the Middle East. In 14 countries Christians are barred from proselytising, and in 12 Muslims are banned from converting to Christianity. There are 11 states in which Christians in public schools have to take classes in Islam, and six in which Muslims are given preference over Christians in custody cases.

Aside from that there has also been a perception that in the task of building integration, public space in some Middle Eastern contexts has been significantly Islamized. Andreas Bandak, reflecting on the period 2004–2010, discussed the changing nature of space in Damascus, which had seen a serious increase in mosque building, and the use of ever more intrusive audio-visual aids, such as neon lights and loudspeakers to ever more boldly assert the place of Islam as the dominant societal presence and the consequent sidelining of minority groups.[20] This is an observation which holds true in a number of others states, notably Jordan.

We can conclude from this that policies based heavily around assimilation have the potential to serious hurt the place of Christians, and in any context carry the possibility of despotic tendencies and serious discrimination. In attempting to ensure

---

19   Fox, J. (2008) *A World Survey of Religion and the State*. New York: Cambridge University Press and Fox (2013).
20   Bandak, A. (2014) 'Of refrains and rhythms in contemporary Damascus urban space and Christian–Muslim coexistence.' *Current Anthropology 55* S10, The Anthropology of Christianity: Unity, Diversity, New Directions (December), S248–S261.

the homogeneity of the community, the temptation is either to exclude migrants and minorities, or else force their assimilation at the expense of their own beliefs and practices.

4. Securitization

In common with several of the above responses, securitization is a policy (or set of policies) that reflects a treatment of citizenship and migrants entirely from the perspective of state interest. In this case, migrants are assessed in terms of the risk they pose as a direct security threat, more than the more cultural threat of undermining homogeneity that underpins the assimilation tactic. In many Western states this agenda has come to define migration policy, particularly in relation to accepting refugees from the Middle East. The executive order signed by President Trump soon after entering office that bans refugees and migrants from states including Syria, Yemen and Iran among others is the most prominent and extreme version of this agenda.

While recognizing that states do have a duty to protect their own citizens it is clear that, much like the market state approach, this agenda falls into the trap of de-humanizing and de-personalizing migrants. There is no good reason to assume that all people from these countries pose a blanket risk to the safety of American citizens. In addition, a securitizing agenda leads to understandable feelings of resentment among migrant groups, and can impact upon their ability to feel integrated into society.

Each of these approaches, as we have seen, raises challenges for a Christian vision of citizenship and the devising of migration policy.

A NOTE ON REFUGEES

This chapter has so far looked at migrants in general. It is estimated that of the total world population of migrants (people living outside the country of their birth) a little under 10 per cent are refugees.[21] The prominence of the current refugee crisis, made more visible by a global mass media, is such that it can come to dominate the whole discourse around migration. It is worth

---

21   UN DESA (2015).

briefly dealing with the specific issue of refugees, because policy in that area provides some clear examples of the way in which the tactics discussed above have worked out in practice.

For example, there is a presumption that the locus of political identity is the state. The state confers citizenship to individuals, whose legal and civic identity is defined accordingly. Within that paradigm refugees present a problem. As people who have either rejected or been rejected by their own state they become stateless individuals. Since states are supposed to provide citizenship and to guarantee the rights and status of individuals, an individual without a state is uniquely vulnerable.

This is in turn related to a second issue, which is that, as with migration more broadly, the debate is centred around the interests of states and the security agenda. Refugee policy across the West has been more and more centred on the issues of what states can afford to do, and what risks are entailed in taking on refugees. Notable in this is the trend of de-humanizing or de-personalizing refugees, and a downgrading of ideas of justice and the needs of individuals in favour of a state-interest led model.

The trend of de-humanizing the issue is also apparent in the way in which the system as a whole seems purpose built to deter human agency and dignity. A narrative has been created that divides refugees into 'good' and 'bad' sets.[22] 'Good' refugees are those that stay in camps and wait to be processed. They are the passive recipients of care from other states and ought to wait until they have been deemed sufficiently acceptable to a state's interest to be permitted access. By contrast 'bad' refugees are those that do not wait in the conditions of the camps but make an effort to help themselves through their own agency by trying to travel to a new country of their own choosing, perhaps by attempting to cross the Mediterranean. These 'bad' refugees are deemed to be jumping the queue, and are particularly likely to be subject to fears stemming from the securitization agenda. In a sense this reiterates the extent to which debates over migration have become excessively focused on the interests of states and the de-humanizing of migrants, whether refugees or not.

---

22   Mavelli, L. and Wilson, E. (eds) (2017) *The Refugee Crisis and Religion*. London: Rowman & Littlefield.

TOWARDS A NEW DISTINCTIVELY CHRISTIAN ANSWER

This chapter has thus far been critical of the classic approaches of states towards managing migrants and granting citizenship. Against the construction of the market state, with migrants viewed as commodified labour, it argued that such an approach de-humanized migrants, led to an undermining of human dignity and put economic productivity on a pedestal above a Christian understanding of labour.

Against the policies of assimilation, it argued that such policies can easily come to be discriminatory or even despotic. In a Middle Eastern context, this can have particularly difficult consequences for Christians. In both cases, and particularly seen when considering the situation of refugees, the interest and security of the state has come to thoroughly dominate the entire discourse. These approaches fall short of a Christian answer to the issues. There are, however, some building blocks on which to construct a better way forwards. The first is a need for a re-emphasis on humanity and human dignity at the heart of all such policies. The second is to re-configure the balancing act between the rights owed to people and the responsibilities owed by them. A final theme is the need to look again at the Christian model of the Common Good and to propose a way forwards that moves beyond an identity that ends at the border.

1. A humanized model

The first and critical principle for a new Christian model is that any and all approaches to the question of citizenship or migration policy must start from the simple position that those involved are human beings imbued with human dignity. This simple message is critical to any genuinely Christian model of politics or society and is far too often overlooked in current policy.

Christian anthropology rests on the principle that all humans are made in the image of God (Genesis 1.27 'So God created mankind in his own image' and Genesis 9.6 'for in the image of God has God made mankind'). Furthermore, the equal dignity of humanity is established in a salvation which is not limited by any racial, gender or social status (Galatians 3.28; Revelation 7.9).

The special status of humanity, made in the image of God, demands that we treat one another in the same light – as equally imbued with an essential dignity and a special status in the eyes of God.

As such the reduction of human beings to nothing more than economic units, or commodities, is an affront to the idea of human dignity. In place of the recognition of humanity the approaches of the market state, in particular, tend towards an idolatrous obsession with economic progress at the expense of human dignity. Pope Francis's Encyclical *Evangelii Gaudium* powerfully argues that

> The worship of the ancient golden calf (cf. Exodus 32.1–35) has returned in a new and ruthless guise in the idolatry of money and the dictatorship of an impersonal economy lacking a truly human purpose. The worldwide crisis affecting finance and the economy lays bare their imbalances and, above all, their lack of real concern for human beings; man is reduced to one of his needs alone: consumption.[23]

The point about recognizing human dignity naturally takes on particular importance in the case of refugees. As argued above the system of many states currently seems to actively deny any dignity or agency to refugees themselves, leaving them as nothing more than a security threat or an economic commodity to be assessed by states.

2. The balance between rights and responsibilities

Having established the need for a model of citizenship and the treatment of migrants which prioritizes human dignity, there is a need to establish what that might look like in practice. Most debates around citizenship ultimately come down to a clash between a communitarian approach which stresses the need for responsibilities on citizens[24] and an individualist approach that stresses a rights model.[25]

23 Pope Francis (2013) *Evangelii Gaudium*. https://w2.vatican.va/content/francesco/
    en/apost_exhortations/documents/papa-francesco_esortazione-ap_20131124_
    evangelii-gaudium.html, accessed on 22 March 2017.
24 For example, Shafir, G. (1998) *The Citizenship Debates: A Reader.* Minneapolis, MN:
    University of Minnesota Press.
25 For example, Rawls, J. (1972) *A Theory of Justice.* Oxford: Oxford University Press.

The advantage of a rights model is that it recognizes the dignity of each human being and defines their rights as an individual. There are, of course, a number of international human rights treaties which affect the status of individuals and which might serve as models for an extension of the system. For example, the UN Convention Relating to the Status of Refugees guarantees the rights of anyone claiming asylum, preventing them from being expelled (Article 32) or forcibly returned (Article 33) and guaranteeing, among other things, their freedom of religion (Article 4). This convention has 145 signatories. It is notable that a number of Middle Eastern states, including Saudi Arabia, Iraq, Jordan, Oman and the UAE, are not signatories to the Convention. It should be noted that this is not a simplistic criticism of Islamic majority countries. Four out of the five biggest hosts for refugees worldwide are Islamic majority counties.[26]

Similarly, in the case of migrant workers, a possible model lies in the International Convention on the Protection of the Rights of All Migrant Workers and Members of their Families. Its scope is limited, not least because it has only 38 signatories of whom only Syria, Turkey and Egypt are Middle Eastern states.

There is a model in international law, therefore, for an extension of the human rights model. There is also a strong biblical basis for a more rights-based approach. On the topic of migrants in particular the Old Testament has a fairly developed set of rights which it attaches to the *gerim* (sojourners, settled foreigners). Among other things there is a clear prohibition against abuse of foreigners (Leviticus 19.33–34), a call for equal treatment of foreigners before the law (Leviticus 24.22; Deuteronomy 1.16) and the call for those who have integrated into the community to be included in the feasts and festivals of Israel (Exodus 12.48; Deuteronomy 31.12).

There are dangers in over-emphasizing the importance of rights. Human beings are body, mind and soul, and their political and civic identity reflects that in so far as a rights-based model of citizenship appeals most to the mind – it is the logical, and legal, sense of being protected and guaranteed a particular status. A more communitarian model might view citizenship more as

---

26   Zaman (2017).

a matter of the soul – of real essential belonging to a place and, therefore, what a citizen owes to the state. This mind against soul battle for the authentic nature of citizenship has always characterized the debate.[27]

Just as rights have a strong Christian pedigree in talking about citizenship, so too the more communitarian approach can claim a Christian heritage. In a 2001 essay Archbishop Vincent Nichols argued that '"Solidarity" is the Christian word for citizenship'.[28] In seeking a balance, however, too many states at present have over-emphasized the responsibilities due of migrants and minorities in particular, with the interest of the state having come to excessively outweigh the dignity of individual people.

3. The common good beyond state borders

The difficulty in rebalancing the scales between individual rights and collective responsibility lies in the continuing role of states as the ultimate arbiters of citizenship. If rights are only defined according to the state then there is a clear potential contest between the state's own interests (in terms of the securitization or market needs discussed above) and the interests of individuals seeking citizenship. The only effective means to guarantee a more Christian conception of citizenship that prioritizes human dignity over state economic pressures is with a more extensive and robust international legal framework.

This can be overstated. There is no need to move all the way to a fully cosmopolitan system that precludes all sense of national borders. The Old Testament demands for the legal rights of sojourners never amount to total equality with Israelites. Sojourners could not, for example, become king (Deuteronomy 17.15). Nor does a rights-based approach entirely solve the issue of state interests – since in practice, acting to protect these rights will still require states as agents.

However, it is to argue that an extension of international law to guarantee a minimum level of working rights, and to resist

---

27 See, for example, Stapleton, J. (2005) 'Citizenship versus patriotism in twentieth-century England.' *The Historical Journal 48*, 1, 151–178.
28 Nichols, V. (2001) 'The Common Good.' In D. Alton (ed.) *Citizen 21: Citizenship in the New Millennium.* London: HarperCollins.

the social, political, civic and cultural exclusion felt by migrants in particular, and minority groups in general, across too many countries, is long overdue. Breaking the model of the nation-state as the locus of all political and civic identity is essential in this. As long as citizenship is envisaged only as a filing system for dividing people according to state authority the problems outlined above will continue.[29]

In this way, the responsibilities of citizens can still be emphasized and encouraged. States ought certainly to be mindful of protecting themselves from dangerous elements. Citizens ought to work to contribute towards the common good and to attempt to integrate into wider society. A rights-based model in fact can aid that process of integration. With a fuller set of rights to participate in all aspects of society, whether as a migrant worker or as a minority group within a country, more opportunities for integration can emerge. Instead of creating a stratified society with an underclass who lack the ability to work in some areas, manifest their beliefs or participate in civic and political life, a freer society can provide opportunities for more rapid and lasting integration.[30]

A model of citizenship underpinned by an international human rights model has much to recommend it in Christian terms, not least in nuancing the idea of neighbourliness beyond state and ethnic boundaries. The question 'who is my neighbour?' (Luke 10.29) is a critical question in citizenship. Jesus' answer is to provide the parable of the Good Samaritan. However else that parable is to be understood, one point that seems incontestable is that neighbourliness goes beyond the bounded community. Samaritans and Jews are different peoples, yet the responsibility of care transcends that difference.

CONCLUSION

This chapter has argued that a Christian conception of citizenship for a new age demands a break from the state-centred model that currently dominates, in favour of a more human-centred model

---

29   Brubaker, R. (1992) *Citizenship and Nationhood in France and Germany*. Cambridge, MA: Harvard University Press.
30   Maxwell (2010).

with an international legal framework. It is fair to say that such a vision demands a radical change which is beyond the abilities of individuals to create.

This is all the more true within a Middle Eastern context. Only a minority of Middle East states are signatories to treaties on refugees or migrant workers. A majority are among the most oppressive states in terms of restrictions on religious freedom. Minority and migrant groups across much of the region are under enormous pressure. Several religious and ethnic groups have all but vanished.[31]

Accordingly, progress on these issues requires more than individuals are able to provide. It will require a genuine international response, inspired by solidarity, to resolve a set of interlinked issues (citizenship, the refugee crisis, the status of migrant workers, religious freedom, human rights) that are causing a global crisis. The Christian contribution towards such a response must lie in the promotion of a vision of citizenship based on more than states, and with the indispensable value of human dignity at its heart.

---

31   Russell (2014).

CONCLUSION

One of the findings of the substantial study on *Citizenship in Britain: Values, Participation and Democracy* was that those individuals who regarded themselves as belonging to a particular religion often exhibited atypical characteristics.[1] Such people recorded comparatively high levels of interpersonal trust, of trust in the police, of respect for the law and of a citizen's duty to vote. They also recorded higher than average levels of group membership, of engagement in informal activities, of political participation and of time 'donation'. It is people of religious faith who are often the most active in rebuilding broken communities. Faith seems to make us better and more actively engaged citizens. Faith is often regarded as the engine that drives a great deal of the social and political activism taking place in the culture. In spite of belonging to a community of heavenly citizenship which awaits a new Kingdom that is not of this world, the Christians are not passive citizens of our earthly societies. The Church is often the first in and last out in many of our most deprived communities.

In this book, the authors have depicted a biblical vision of citizenship that makes active participation in the life of the community our calling and priority. Moreover, they highlighted the reasons why such active participation should be hopeful and constructive, providing timely and relevant impetus to the rebuilding of broken communities, efforts at peace in societies facing conflict, and creative alternatives at generating solidarity in discriminating circumstances. As highlighted here, a biblical vision of citizenship chooses neither withdrawal from civic engagement nor immersion or assimilation, but a critical engagement with the political establishment. This was evidenced

---

1   Pattie, C., Seyd, P. and Whiteley, P. (2004) *Citizenship in Britain: Values, Participation and Democracy.* Cambridge: Cambridge University Press.

in the context of the Middle East, where critical engagement with the political establishment means unmasking and shaming the real agendas of Western democracies' dealings with Arab states and alliances with religiously fundamentalist groups which have had a destabilizing effect for the Christian communities in the region. However, it also means that despite persecution, destruction and population reduction, the Christian message of service, love and forgiveness will continue to undergird a Christian identity and view of citizenship.

Much more has been written and could be said about the Middle East and the plight of the Christians there; however, it is important to recognize that in this book we have provided a series of perspectives that have in common the Bible as the central source of wisdom and as the foundation on which the Christian communities are built and which shapes their identity and view of citizenship. This means that a biblical vision of citizenship for the Middle East or any other place where Christian communities are under threat needs to support the establishment of societies based on rights, responsibilities and human dignity over and above particular interests of the states, their economic demands or security agendas. To make a biblical case for citizenship is to challenge those interests and ensure that citizens of all confessions, ethnicities or religions are equally protected and respected and allowed to thrive as active and engaged citizens of their nations.

REFERENCES

Anderson, B. (1991) *Imagined Communities: Reflections on the Origin and Spread of Nationalism*, rev. ed. London and New York: Verso.

Anderson, R.S. (2007) *Something Old, Something New: Marriage and Family Ministry in a Postmodern Culture*. Eugene, OR: Wipf and Stock Publishers.

Augustine, City of God, XIV. ch.4, pp.300–302.

Ath. Pol. 57.3

Awad, N.G. (2012a) *And Freedom Became a Public-Square: Political, Sociological and Religious Overview on the Arab Christians and the Arabic Spring*. Berlin and Zürich: LIT Verlag.

Awad, N.G. (2012b) 'Man Ḥaūwala al-Ṭaūrah as-Sūriyya īlā Sāḥat Maʻrakah wa-Limāḏā?' (Who Transformed the Syrian Revolution into a Battle-Zone and Why?) *al-Aūwān*, 27 November. Available at http://bit.ly/2qAAEuG, accessed on 6 March 2016.

Awad, N.G. (2012c) 'Īʻādat Qirāʼa ll-Ḥārīṭah: Man maʻ Māḏā wa li-Māḏā?' (Re-Reading the Map: Who with What and Why?) *al-Mustaqbal Newpaper*, 24 June. Available at www.almustaqbal.com/v4/Article. aspx?Type=np&Articleid=527429, accessed on 21 March 2017.

Awad, N.G. (2013a) 'The Christians and the Syrian Revolution: Which Fears from the Rebellion? Which Political System in the Future?' In M. Raheb (ed.) *The Arabic Spring and the Christians of the Middle East*. Bethlehem: Diyar Publishers.

Awad, N.G. (2013b) 'Il faut sauver les chrétiens de Syrie, mais de quoi?' *Le Monde*, 17 September. Available at www.lemonde.fr/idees/article/2013/09/17/il-faut-sauver-les-chretiens-de-syrie-mais-de-quoi_3479209_3232.html, accessed on 21 March 2017.

Awad, N.G. (2014a) 'Is secularity by any means imaginable? A reading of the idea of "civil state" in the Syrian Muslim Brotherhood's contemporary political project for the Syria of the future.' *Islamochristiana 40*, 105–124.

Awad, N.G. (2014b) '"an "Ḥimāyat al-Aqaliyyāt" wal-Massīḥiyyīn fī al-Masʼālah As-Sūriyya.' (On 'Minorities-Protection' and the Christians in the Syrian Case.) *Almustaqbal Newspaper*, 2 February. Available at www.almustaqbal.com/v4/Article.aspx?Type=np&Articleid=604364, accessed on 21 March 2017.

Awad, N.G. (2014c) 'Theologian: Minority in Syria is Democrats, Liberals from All Religions.' *Syria Direct*, 21 May. Available at www.syriadirect.org/news/theologian-minority-in-syria-is-democrats-liberals-of-all-religions, accessed on 21 March 2017.

Awad, N.G. (2015a) 'Muǧtamaʿāt Madaniyya Muʾlmanah: Ahūa Mumkin am Ḥulm ʿAṣṣī ʿan at-Taḥqīq?' (Secularized Civil Societies: Is it Possible or Impossible?) *Al-Ǧadīd Magazine*, 12 January. Available at www.aljadeedmagazine.com/?id=1138, accessed on 21 March 2017.

Awad, N.G. (2015b) 'Kaī Lā Nūwaṣṣif Ḥaṭaʾan mā Yaḥuṭ wa Limāḍā Ḥadaṭa fī Sūrīyyā!!' (Lest We Misread What Happens and Why Did it Happen in Syria!!) *al-Mustaqbal Newspaper*, 19 April. Available at www.almustaqbal.com/v4/Article.aspx?Type=NP&ArticleID=657817, accessed on 21 March 2017.

Awad, N.G. (2016) 'Lā Ufuq ll-Ḥuḍūr al-Masīḥī fī Sūriyyā' (No Horizon to the Christian Presence in Syria). *Al-ʿArabī al-Ǧadīd Newspaper*, 6 February. Available at https://www.alaraby.co.uk/opinion/2016/2/6/%D9%84%D8%A7-%D8%A3%D9%81%D9%82-%D9%84%D9%84%D8%AD%D8%B6%D9%88%D8%B1-%D8%A7%D9%84%D9%85%D8%B3%D9%8A%D8%AD%D9%8A-%D9%81%D9%8A-%D8%B3%D9%88%D8%B1%D9%8A%D8%A9, accessed on 2 May 2017.

Bandak, A. (2014) 'Of refrains and rhythms in contemporary Damascus urban space and Christian–Muslim coexistence'. *Current Anthropology 55*, S10, The Anthropology of Christianity: Unity, Diversity, New Directions, S248–S261.

Barth, K. (1961) *Church Dogmatics, 4 vols, Vol. III, 'The Doctrine of Creation', Part 4, 'The Command of God the Creator'.* Edinburgh: T. & T. Clark.

Battistella, R.G. (2008) 'Migration and Human Dignity: From Policies of Exclusion to Policies Based on Human Rights.' In D.G. Groody and G. Campese (eds) *A Promised Land, A Perilous Journey: Theological Perspectives on Migration.* Notre Dame, IN: University of Notre Dame Press.

Biggar, N. (2011) 'Melting the icepacks of enmity: Forgiveness and reconciliation in Northern Ireland.' *Studies in Christian Ethics 24*, 2, 200–204.

Bin Talal, H. (1994) *Christianity in the Arab World*. Amman: Royal Institute for Inter-Faith Studies.

Bockmuehl, M. (1994) *This Jesus*. London: T. & T. Clark.

Bonhoeffer, D. (2008) *Ethics, Vol. 6*. Minneapolis, MN: Fortress Press.

Bonner, B., Ener, M. and Singer, A. (2003) *Poverty and Charity in Middle Eastern Contexts*. Albany, NY: SUNY Press.

Borrut, A. and Donner, F.M. (2016) 'Introduction: Christians and Others in the Umayyad State.' In A. Borrut and F.M. Donner (eds) *Christians and Others in the Umayyad State*, LAMINE 1 (Late Antique and Medieval Islamic Near East, number 1). Chicago, IL: The Oriental Institute of the University of Chicago.

Borrut, A. and Donner, F.M. (eds) (2016) *Christians and Others in the Umayyad State*, LAMINE 1 (Late Antique and Medieval Islamic Near East, number 1). Chicago, IL: The Oriental Institute of the University of Chicago.

Brague, R. (2009) 'Assyrians Contributions to the Islamic Civilisation.' Available at www.christiansofiraq.com/assyriancontributionstotheislamic civilisation.htm, accessed on 9 September 2016.

Brague, R. (2009) The Legend of the Middle Ages, 2009, p.164. Retrieved 9 September, 2016.

Brock, S.P. (1982) 'Transformations of the Edessa Portrait.' In G.H.A. Juynboll (ed.) *Studies in the First Century of Islamic Society*, Papers on Islamic History 5. Carbondale, IL: Southern Illinois University Press.

Brubaker, R. (1992) *Citizenship and Nationhood in France and Germany.* Cambridge, MA: Harvard University Press.

Brueggemann, W. (1997) *Theology of the Old Testament.* Minneapolis, MN: Fortress Press.

Brueggemann, W. (2001) *Peace: Living toward a Vision.* St. Louis, MO: Chalice Press.

Brueggemann, W. (2004) 'Scripture: Old Testament.' In P. Scott and W.T. Cavanaugh (eds) *The Blackwell Companion to Political Theology*, Blackwell Companions to Religion. Oxford: Blackwell.

Buijs, G. (2008) 'Agapé and the Origins of Civil Society.' In H. Geertsema, R. Peels and J. van der Stoep (eds) *Philosophy Put to Work: Contemporary Issues in Arts, Society, Politics, Science and Religion.* Amsterdam: VU University.

Casey, L. (2016) 'The Casey Review: A Review into Opportunity and Integration (Executive Summary).' London: Department for Communities and Local Government.

Clarke, P.P. (2013) 'Citizenship.' In P.P. Clarke and A. Linzey (eds) *Dictionary of Ethics, Theology and Society.* Abingdon: Routledge.

Clements, K. (1986) *True Patriotism: Love of Country in Dialogue with the Witness of Dietrich Bonhoeffer.* London: Collins.

Colley, L. (2005) *Britons: Forging the Nation, 1707–1837.* New Haven, CT: Yale University Press.

Colson, E. (2003) 'Forced migration and the anthropological response.' *Journal of Refugee Studies 16*, 1, 1–18.

Davison Hunter, J. (2010) *To Change the World: The Irony, Tragedy, and Possibility of Christianity in the Late Modern World.* Oxford: Oxford University Press.

Debié, M. (2016) 'Christians in the Service of the Caliph: Through the Looking Glass of Communal Identities.' In A. Borrut and F.M. Donner (eds) *Christians and Others in the Umayyad State*, LAMINE 1 (Late Antique and Medieval Islamic Near East, number 1). Chicago, IL: The Oriental Institute of the University of Chicago.

Dockery, D.S. (2008) *Renewing Minds: Serving Church and Society through Christian Higher Education, Revised and Updated.* Nashville, TN: B&H Publishing Group.

Ehrenberg, V. (1968) *From Solon to Socrates: Greek History and Civilization during the 6th and 5th Centuries BC.* London: Methuen.

El-Haj, A. (2009) 'Becoming citizens in an era of globalization and transnational migration: Re-imagining citizenship as critical practice.' *Theory into Practice* 48, 4, 274–282.

Extramiana, C. and Van Avermaet, P. (2011) 'Language requirements for adult migrants in Council of Europe member states: Report on a survey.' Strasbourg: Council of Europe, Language Policy Division.

Fichte, J.G. (1922) *Addresses to the German Nation*. Chicago, IL: Open Court Press.

Fisher Merrill, A. and Calhoun, H.J. () The world's great dailies: profiles of fifty newspapers, LA University of Michigan.

Fox, J. (2008) *A World Survey of Religion and the State*. New York: Cambridge University Press.

Fox, J. (2013) *An Introduction to Religion and Politics: Theory and Practice*. Oxford: Routledge.

Goodhart, D. (2013) *The British Dream. Successes and Failures of Post-War Immigration*. London: Atlantic Books.

Greengrass, M. (2013) *Christendom Destroyed: Europe 1517–1648*. St Ives: Penguin.

Griffith, S.H. (2016) 'The Manṣūr Family and Saint John of Damascus: Christians and Muslims in Umayyad Times.' In A. Borrut and F.M. Donner (eds) *Christians and Others in the Umayyad State*, LAMINE 1 (Late Antique and Medieval Islamic Near East, number 1). Chicago, IL: The Oriental Institute of the University of Chicago.

Harpsfield, N. (1932) *The Life and Death of Sir Thomas Moore, Knight, Sometymes Lord High Chancellor of England*. E.V. Hitchcock and R.W. Chambers (eds), Early English Text Society, Original Series no. 186. London: Oxford University Press.

Harrak, A. (2015) 'Dionysius of Tell-Maḥrē: Patriarch, Diplomat and an Inquisitive Chronicler.' In M. Doerffer, E. Fiano and K. Smith (eds) *Syriac Encounters: Papers from the Sixth North American Syriac Symposium*. Leuven: Peeters.

Harris, E.M. (2016) 'A note on adoption and deme registration.' *TYCHE – Contributions to Ancient History, Papyrology and Epigraphy 11*, 1, 5.

Hastings, A. (1997) *The Construction of Nationhood: Ethnicity, Religion, and Nationalism*. Cambridge: Cambridge University Press.

Hengel, M. and Deines, R. (1991) *The Pre-Christian Paul*. Philadelphia: Trinity Press International.

Henson, H. (1936) *Christian Morality: Natural, Developing, Final, Gifford Lectures 1935–36*. Oxford: Clarendon Press.

Hill, D. (1993) *Islamic Science and Engineering*. Edinburgh: Edinburgh University Press.

Hoffmeier, J.K. (1983) 'Some Thoughts on Genesis 1 & 2 and Egyptian Cosmology.' Available at www.academia.edu/2118837/Some_Thoughts_on_Genesis_1_and_2_and_Egyptian_Cosmology, accessed on 20 March 2017.

Howe, S. (2002) *Empire: A Very Short Introduction*. Oxford: Oxford University Press.

Humphrey, M. (1993) 'Migrants, workers and refugees: The political economy of population movements in the Middle East.' *Middle East Report 181*, Radical Movements: Migrants, Workers and Refugees, 2–7.

Jackson Preece, J. (2005) *Minority Rights.* Cambridge: Polity Press.

Jefford, C.N. (2013) *The Epistle to Diognetus (with the Fragment of Quadratus).* Oxford: Oxford University Press.

Kaser, K. (2011) *The Balkans and the Near East: Introduction to a Shared History.* Berlin: Lit Verlag.

Kere, A. and Bell, R. (2017) 'All Party Parliamentary Group on Social Integration: Interim Report into Integration of Immigrants.' Available at www.socialintegrationappg.org.uk/reports, accessed on 11 February 2017.

Kerr, D.A. (2003) 'A Western Christian Appreciation of the Eastern Christianity.' In B.J. Bailey and J.M. Bailey (eds) *Who Are the Christians in the Middle East?* Grand Rapids, MI/Cambridge, UK: Eerdmans.

Lacocque, A. (2015) *The Book of Daniel.* Eugene, OR: Wipf and Stock Publishers.

Lang, M.G. (ed.) (2011) *Christian Peace and Nonviolence: A Documentary History.* Maryknoll, NY: Orbis Books.

Lattouf, M. (2004) *Women, Education, and Socialization in Modern Lebanon: 19th and 20th Centuries Social History.* Lanham, MD: University Press of America.

Manville, P.B. (2014) *The Origins of Citizenship in Ancient Athens.* Princeton, NJ: Princeton University Press.

Maurice, F.D. (1893) *Social Morality.* London: Macmillan.

Mavelli, L. and Wilson, E. (eds) (2017) *The Refugee Crisis and Religion.* London: Rowman & Littlefield.

Maxwell, R. (2010) 'Evaluating migrant integration: Political attitudes across generations in Europe.' *The International Migration Review 44*, 1, 25–52.

Mazower, M. (2001) *The Balkans: From the End of Byzantium to the Present Day.* London: Phoenix Press.

Meeks, W. (2003) *The First Urban Christians: The Social World of the Apostle Paul.* New Haven, CT: Yale University Press.

Miller, D. (1995) *On Nationality.* Oxford: Clarendon Press.

Miller, M.E. and Gengrich, B.N. (eds) (1994) *The Church's Peace Witness.* Cambridge, MA: Eerdmans.

Miller, R. (2001) 'Christian Attitudes towards Boundaries.' In D. Miller and S. Hashmi (eds) *Boundaries and Justice: Diverse Ethical Perspectives.* Princeton, NJ: Princeton University Press.

Nichols, V. (2001) 'The Common Good.' In D. Alton (ed.) *Citizen 21: Citizenship in the New Millennium.* London: HarperCollins.

Nygren, A. (1982) *Agape and Eros*, trans. Philip S. Watson. Chicago: University of Chicago Press.

O'Donovan, O. (1986) *The Desire of the Nations: Rediscovering the Roots of Political Theology.* Cambridge: Cambridge University Press.

O'Donovan, O. (1999) *The Desire of the Nations: Rediscovering the Roots of Political Theology.* Cambridge: Cambridge University Press.

Ohmae, K. (1995) *The End of the Nation State: The Rise of Regional Economies.* New York, NY: Simon & Schuster.

Parthasarathi, P. and Quayaert, D. (2011) 'Migrant workers in the Middle East: Introduction'. *International Labor and Working-Class History 79*, 1, 4–6.

Pattie, C., Seyd, P. and Whiteley, P. (2004) *Citizenship in Britain: Values, Participation and Democracy.* Cambridge: Cambridge University Press.

Pew Research Centre, Religion and Public Life (2015) 'The Future of World Religions: Population Growth Projections, 2010–2050.' Available at www.pewforum.org/2015/04/02/religious-projections-2010-2050, accessed on 22 March 2017.

Picirilli, R.E. (1986) *Paul the Apostle.* Chicago, IL: Moody Publishers.

Pilch, J.J.A. (2012) *Cultural Handbook to the Bible.* Grand Rapids, MI: William. B. Eerdmans Publishing.

Plantinga Jr., C. (1995) *Not the Way It's Supposed to Be: A Breviary of Sin.* Grand Rapids, MI: Eerdmans.

Pope Francis (2013) *Evangelii Gaudium.* Available at https://w2.vatican.va/content/francesco/en/apost_exhortations/documents/papa-francesco_esortazione-ap_20131124_evangelii-gaudium.html, accessed on 22 March 2017.

Pope Francis (2016) 'Meeting with World of Labour.' Speech delivered at Bachilleres College, State of Chihuahua, Ciudad Juárez. 17 February.

Ravitsky, A. (1987) 'Peace.' In A. Cohen and P. Mendes-Flohr (eds) *Contemporary Jewish Religious Thought.* New York: Charles Scribner's Sons.

Rawls, J. (1972) *A Theory of Justice.* Oxford: Oxford University Press.

Ritivoi, A.D. (2002) *Yesterday's Self: Nostalgia and the Immigrant Identity.* Lanham, MD: Rowman & Littlefield Publishers.

Romocea, C. and Girma, M. (eds) (2015) *Democracy, Conflict and the Bible.* Swindon: Bible Society.

Ruano, E.B. and Burgos, M.E. (1992) *17e Congrès international des sciences historiques: Madrid, du 26 août au 2 septembre 1990.* Madrid: Comité international des sciences historiques.

Russell, G. (2014) *Heirs to Forgotten Kingdoms: Journeys into the Disappearing Religions of the Middle East.* London: Simon & Schuster.

Ryrie, C.C. (2017) *Protestants: The Faith that Made the Modern World.* London: Penguin.

Sacks, J. (1997) *Faith in the Future.* Macon, GA: Mercer University Press.

Schnelle, U. (2005) *Apostle Paul: His Life and Theology.* Ada, MI: Baker Academic.

Shafir, G. (1998) *The Citizenship Debates: A Reader.* Minneapolis, MN: University of Minnesota Press.

Siedentop, L. (2014) *Inventing the Individual: The Origins of Western Liberalism.* Cambridge, MA: Harvard University Press.

Skillen, J.W. (2014) *The Good of Politics (Engaging Culture): A Biblical, Historical, and Contemporary Introduction.* Ada, MI: Baker Academic.

Smith, J. (2015) 'Muslim-Christian Relations: Historical and Contemporary Realities.' Available at http://religion.oxfordre.com/view/10.1093/acrefore/9780199340378.001.0001/acrefore-9780199340378-e-11, accessed on 17 August 2016.

Snyder, S. (2011) 'Globalization: Challenges to Christianity.' *Journal of World Christianity 4*, 1, 44–54.

Stapleton, J. (2005) 'Citizenship versus patriotism in twentieth-century England.' *The Historical Journal 48*, 1, 151–178.

Stefanovic, Z. (2007) *Daniel: Wisdom to the Wise: Commentary on the Book of Daniel.* Nampa, ID: Pacific Press Publishing.

Stone, E. (1997) 'City-states and their Centres.' Miller, R. (2001) 'Christian Attitudes towards Boundaries.' In D.L. Nichols and T.H. Charlton (eds). *The Archaeology of City-States: Cross-Cultural Approaches.* Washington, DC: Smithsonian Institution Press.

Sutherland, P.D. (2008) 'A golden mean between multiculturalism and assimilation.' *Studies: An Irish Quarterly Review 97*, 385, 73–86.

Taylor, C. (2007) *A Secular Age.* Cambridge, MA: Harvard University Press.

Taylor, C. (2009) 'Foreword: What is Secularism?' In G.B. Levey and T. Modood (eds) *Secularism, Religion and Multicultural Citizenship.* Cambridge and New York: Cambridge University Press.

Teague, M. (2010) 'The new Christian question.' *Al Jadid Magazine 16*, 62.

Temple, W. (1928) *Christianity and the State, Henry Scott Holland Memorial Lectures 1928.* London: Macmillan.

UN DESA (2015) *International Migration Report 2015.* Available at www.un.org/en/development/desa/population/migration/publications/migrationreport/docs/MigrationReport2015.pdf, accessed on 22 March 2017.

van De Beek, A. (2008) 'Christian Identity is Identity in Christ.' In E. Van der Borght (ed.) *Christian Identity.* Leiden: Brill.

von Moltke, H.J. (1991) *Letters to Freya: A Witness against Hitler.* London: Collins Harvill.

Valognes, J.P. (1994) *Vie et mort des Chrétiens d' Orient.* Paris: Foyard. p.18; as cited in O'Mahoney, A. (2009) 'Christianity in Iraq: Modern History, Theology, Dialogue and Politics (Until 2003),' in E.C.D. Hunter (ed.) *The Christian Heritage of Iraq: Collected Papers from the Christianity of Iraq, I–V Seminar Days.* Piscataway, NJ: Georgias Press, pp.237–284.

Wang, T. (2003) *History of the World.* New York: iUniverse Inc.

Westermann, C. (1984) *Genesis 1–11: A Commentary*, trans. John J. Scullion. London: SPCK.

White, R. (2001) *Love's Philosophy.* Lanham, MD: Rowman & Littlefield Publishers.

Wolterstorff, N. (2008) *Justice: Rights and Wrongs*. Princeton, NJ: Princeton University Press.

Wright, N.T. (2002) 'The Letter to the Romans: Introduction, Commentary, and Reflections.' In *The New Interpreters Bible, Vol. X*. Nashville, TN: Abingdon.

Yevtushenko, Y. (1991) 'Babii Yar.' In *The Collected Poems, 1952–90*. Edinburgh: Mainstream Publishing.

Yoder, J.H. (2009) *Christian Attitudes to War, Peace and Revolution*. Grand Rapids, MI: Brazos Press.

Zaman, T. (2017) 'A Right to Neighbourhood: Rethinking Islamic Narratives and Practices of Hospitality in a Sedentarist World.' In L. Mavelli and E. Wilson (eds) *The Refugee Crisis and Religion*. London: Rowman & Littlefield.

Zelnick-Abramovitz, R. (1998) 'Supplication and request: Application by foreigners to the Athenian polis.' *Mnemosyne 51*, 5, 554–573.

CONTRIBUTOR BIOGRAPHIES

Najib George Awad (PhD King's College London and Dr. Theol. Habil. Marburg University) is a professor of Christian Theology and Early/Arab Christianity and the Director of the PhD Program in Hartford Seminary, Connecticut. He is the author of *God without Face? On the Personal Individuation of the Holy Spirit* (Mohr Siebeck, 2011); *And Freedom Became a Public-Square: Political, Sociological and Religious Overviews on the Arab Christians and the Arabic Spring* (LIT Verlag, 2012); and *Orthodoxy in Arabic Terms: A Study of Theodore Abū Qurrah's Trinitarian and Christological Doctrines in an Islamic Context* (De Gruyter, 2015).

Nigel Biggar (PhD University of Chicago) is the Regius Professor of Moral and Pastoral Theology at the University of Oxford, where he also directs the McDonald Centre for Theology, Ethics, and Public Life. Among his publications are *Between Kin and Cosmopolis: An Ethic of the Nation* (James Clarke/Wipf & Stock, 2014); *In Defence of War* (Oxford, 2013); *Behaving in Public: How to Do Christian Ethics* (Eerdmans, 2011); and *Religious Voices in Public Places* (Oxford, 2009). He has also written Op-Ed articles on contemporary issues in the *Irish Times*, *Financial Times*, *Standpoint* magazine, *The Scottish Review*, and in *The Times*.

Issa Diab (DTh University of Strasburg) is a professor of Semitic and Interfaith Studies in Saint Joseph University and the Near East School of Theology in Lebanon. In addition to his expertise in Semitic Studies, Old Testament and Bible Translation, Diab is also a specialist in Middle Eastern Christianity and Islam which includes Semitic Fundamentalism (Christianity, Islam and Judaism). He is the author of numerous books including *The Main Axes in the History of the Eastern Churches and their Relationship with Islam* (forthcoming, 2017); *Environment in the Abrahamic*

Religions (2016); *Introduction to the History and Doctrines of Judaism* (2015); and *Religious Fundamentalism and Fanaticism in Christianity and Islam* (2014). All these books are in Arabic and published by Dar al-Mashreq, Beirut.

Mohammed Girma (PhD Free University of Amsterdam) is an International Advocacy Officer at IBAC and Research Associate at the University of Pretoria. He has previously worked as a research fellow at Yale University and as Assistant Professor of Religious Studies at Evangelical Theological Faculty Leuven, Belgium. He is the author of *Understanding Religion and Social Change in Ethiopia* (Palgrave Macmillan, 2012). He has also written a number of book chapters and articles in peer-reviewed scientific journals.

Cristian Romocea (PhD University of Wales) has also studied for an MPhil degree in International Relations at the University of Cambridge. He is the author of *Church and State: Religious Nationalism and State Identification in Post-communist Romania* (Bloomsbury, 2012) and has edited and written a number of books and articles in various academic journals including *Journal of Church and State, Journal of Legal Studies*, and *Religion, State and Society*.

Ben Ryan is Researcher at the religion and society think tank Theos. He read Theology and Religious Studies at the University of Cambridge and also has an MSc in European Studies from the LSE European Institute. He is the author of a number of reports including *A Soul for the Union* (Theos, 2016) and *Catholic Social Thought and Catholic Charities in Britain Today: Need and Opportunity* (Theos, 2016).

C.A. (Casey) Strine (PhD University of Oxford) is Lecturer in Ancient Near Eastern History and Literature at the University of Sheffield. He is both the author of the award winning monograph *Sworn Enemies* (Walter de Gruyter, 2013) and a contributor to *When the Son of Man Didn't Come: A Constructive Proposal on the Delay of the Parousia*.

SUBJECT INDEX

AUTHOR INDEX